Memories of a *Mad Man*

Stories from the Golden
—and sometimes Tin-Plated—
Age of advertising.

Don Spector

Memories of A Mad Man

By Don Spector

ISBN-10: 1506194346
ISBN-13: 978-1506194349

To my darling Robin

Acknowledgments

After writing millions of words in commercials, ads, brochures, billboards and other media during my advertising career, I was surprised to find that writing this, my first book, was a lot harder than I expected. But I made it through with the encouragement and help of two friends and successful authors, Pancho Kohner and Chris Malburg.

In ad agencies, creating advertising is a team sport with copywriters and art directors working in pairs. I was lucky to have had some excellent art directors as co-creators who share the credit for much of the advertising I talk about in this book. One that stands out was as great a friend as he was an art director, the late Peter Tiisler.

And, of course, through it all my dear wife Robin has been patient, understanding and encouraging.

CONTENTS

∞ 1 ∞

MEET THE MAD "MAD" WORLD

If you ever watched the TV show *Mad Men* you saw me somewhere. The "Mad" in *Mad Men*, of course, stood for Madison Avenue and that's where I started my advertising career about the same time as the show's opening season.

If you did see me in the show I was probably played by an extra in the background because in those early days I was just a lowly mailroom boy. But I was part of the advertising agency scene and I'm impressed by how accurately the producers of the show captured that world—the smoking, the drinking and, yes, the occasional office-based fooling around.

Hopefully, this book will fill in a lot of the blanks in the show that are there because, in large part, they have to make time to run the commercials that are supplied, of course, by those darn advertising agencies.

We didn't know it while we were living them, but the "Mad Men" days were really the "Golden Age" of advertising. The advent of the computer, the Internet, Twitter, Facebook, YouTube and all the other digital assets available today has changed the world of advertising dramatically.

In the "good old days," if we wanted to go to warm California in the dead of a New York winter we could write a TV commercial with palm trees in it and a few weeks later we were shooting on a sunny Southern California beach. Today, the actors can perform on a New York sound stage in front of a blank green backdrop and later a computer can put them on that beach. No traveling, no expense account, no California tan for the writers and art directors who created the spot. (In those days, soaking in the sun to get a good tan was good for you.)

Creative people today are far less likely to enjoy the excitement and pride of seeing their full-color full-page ads in a national magazine. Many of those print ad campaigns have been replaced by company websites, popup ads on web pages and favorable reviews on social media like Facebook and Yelp, many of them planted by hired hands—people paid to write those favorable reviews. These enormous changes are why much of what you'll read about here is written in the past tense. It's how we used to do things…the "old way" and, to a copywriter like me, the better way.

Not that there's anything wrong with all these changes. They can be very effective marketing tools. But, for the most part, they're created and brought to life by people sitting at a computer chained to the Internet. And that doesn't compare to flying jet simulators, diving in shark-filled tanks, traveling to distant places, meeting fascinating people and having often-unforgettable (and often-unrecountable) adventures. That's what we Mad Men—and Mad Women—did. And we got paid pretty well for doing them.

A wit in the old days of radio, Fred Allen, responded to a critic who wrote a devastating review of a piece Allen had written. In a witty public letter, Allen took him to task and, at the end, added a postscript: "...and where were you when the page was blank?"

They're pretty scary things, those blank pages. As a copywriter and, eventually, creative director, at a number of major advertising agencies, I spent many decades facing them and their younger cousins, blank computer screens. Faced with hot deadlines, impatient bosses, hostile clients and, occasionally, a mind as blank as the page I stared at, I managed to fill them with millions of words. Assembled in more or less the right order, those words became thousands of TV commercials, radio spots, newspaper ads, magazine ads, brochures, outdoor boards and matchbook covers.

Many of them have probably annoyed you, but some of them may have convinced you to purchase something. If you've ever bought a bottle of Smirnoff Vodka, a Dodge car, a room at a Ramada Inn or a jar of Pazo Hemorrhoid Cream, I may have been the one who cajoled you into it.

The success of *Mad Men* didn't surprise me. Besides its being a very well-written and well-acted show, the world of advertising has always seemed to fascinate people. That really came home to me once when I was Creative Director of BBDO/West in Los Angeles. I was invited to appear on a popular Los Angeles radio show to talk about advertising.

The first call-in segment was pretty lively with about half of the phone lines lit up. Not bad but my host wanted more action. Off the air during a commercial break, I suggested that he ask me to name one of my agency's ad campaigns.

Back on the air, when he asked, I replied, "We did the 'Ring Around the Collar' ad campaign for Liquid Wisk detergent." In less than one nanosecond, every phone line was flashing red...angry red. For the next hour I was reviled by an army of furious listeners. Callers were offended by the campaign and outraged to think that anyone would be taken in by what they felt was a patronizing and offensive sales pitch. One woman got so mad at me she had to be bleeped several times. Even though, coward that I was, I made it clear that I hadn't created the campaign, the onslaught continued. I actually enjoyed the give-and-take and the host was delighted. Off the air, he commented that it was the biggest phone response he had had in years.

That incident, many years ago, was actually the seed of this book. It proved to me how interested people are in advertising and how much unalloyed joy they take in complaining about it. It's a national sport anyone can play and many do. Consider how often you chat about that really dumb commercial you saw the night before or that funny one you saw during the Super Bowl.

And yet, in spite of protestations by just about every red-blooded American that they absolutely never, ever buy anything because of advertising, they do. That "Ring Around the Collar" campaign for Wisk laundry detergent was fabulously successful, annoying though many people found it...myself included. The "Got Milk" campaign increased milk consumption the first year it appeared by 15%.

That's why I wrote this book...to feed this cobra-and-flute fascination with advertising. It's meant to be entertainment, not a textbook. But on the way through my adventures, you'll learn how traditional advertising was created in the good old days. You'll meet many of the intelligent, eccentric and, often wacko people who created it. And you may come out with a better understanding of why you feel as you do about what some people consider this "monster in our midst."

Advertising is everywhere. It surrounds us like the air we breathe. Sometimes it can be enjoyable but, like air, sometimes it stinks. This book will hopefully explain some of the smiles...as well as the smells.

∞ 2 ∞

PEOPLE: THE FAMOUS, THE NOT SO FAMOUS AND THE INFAMOUS

My greatest joy in advertising has been the people I've dealt with.

My greatest curse in advertising has been the people I've dealt with.

Art directors, copywriters, bosses, composers, clients, actors, musicians, directors, announcers, photographers, authors, account executives, illustrators—I've laughed, cursed, argued, drank, created and debated with them all. They were my favorite part of my hectic world for over four decades.

But before I could get involved with fascinating people like this, I had to get into the business. It wasn't easy and my first effort was a failure… because of a woman. Naturally.

When I entered Hamilton College I had no idea what career to pursue. My dad was a successful doctor and I could probably have stepped into a good practice. But I just wasn't interested in medicine.

Through four years of college earning a B.A. in psychology, no career jumped out at me. Two years earning a Master's in Finance at Columbia didn't seem to help either. So, on graduation day at Columbia, wearing my cap and gown and gripping my degree, I sat there singing the Columbia alma mater, proud but puzzled.

With many of my college buddies well on their way towards

medical degrees and my fellow Finance majors from Columbia commuting to Wall Street jobs every day, I was still racking my brain for the answer to the crucial question: what should I do with my life?

Then one day something struck me. A major theme throughout my education had been writing. I had written for the school newspapers in my high school, my college and my graduate school. And something odd also struck me: every one of those publications was named *The Spectator*. That all three publications should have the same name was certainly a big coincidence. But that their name, *Spectator*, was so similar to my last name, Spector, seemed to be trying to tell me something on the order of "Be a writer, schmuck!"

But what kind of writer? Journalism? Novels? Plays? Movies? Nothing seemed to ring any bells for me…until I read an article about advertising. The more I read, the more the profession seemed to be interesting, dynamic and, watching numerous television commercials featuring well-known personalities, possibly even glamorous. Maybe copywriting was the way to go.

So I set about finding an advertising agency that would hire an inexperienced copywriter. But Madison Avenue wasn't interested. After weeks of non-responsive letter writing and fruitless phone calls, I came up empty.

Then one day a family friend heard of my quandary and told me that he knew someone with a connection to the president of a major Madison Avenue ad agency. At the man's request I went to his home and sat with him as we talked about advertising and my newfound dream of copywritership. His daughter, Cynthia, sat there silently, quietly smiling the whole time.

"Did I have any sales experience?" he asked. Copywriting, he explained, is in reality a form of sales. It would make me more marketable if, in addition to the writing I had done in my school publications, I also had some sales experience on my resumé. He suggested I get a sales job for a month or two after which he would be glad to introduce me to his advertising executive friend.

I applied for a sales job at once-famous Gimbel's department store in midtown Manhattan. The interview seemed to go well. I had always wanted to be in sales, I lied, and thought Gimbel's would be very good place to start.

But there was a problem. My interviewer believed that with my two degrees I was over-qualified for a sales job. He thought I would become dissatisfied quickly and so instead he gave me a job as what they called a section manager.

Armed with a bright fresh Gimbel's-supplied carnation in my sports jacket lapel and a smile on my face, every morning I would help customers and oversee the sales people in the cosmetics and perfume department. It wasn't the sales experience I was looking for but I figured that at least I would observe a lot of sales going on and I could put it on my resume for the advertising executive I would be introduced to.

It was the holiday season so business in the perfume and cosmetics apartment was brisk and so, when possible, I helped make an occasional sale. My claim of sales experience would not be totally bogus.

After two months, I handed in my resignation to Gimbel's and the next day called the gentleman who had promised to introduce me. He wasn't in so I left a message on his answering machine. I got no reply so I called again later. Again no callback. After a few more days of silence, I told my dad about the lack of response and he investigated the situation.

That's when the truth came out. Our family friend who had set me up with my would-be benefactor learned that apparently the man had wanted me to have more than the experience of selling. He had also wanted me to have the experience of asking his daughter out.

That's why she had sat in on our meeting. I could have avoided two months of commuting by subway to Manhattan, walking hard department store floors and dealing with temperamental customers and overtired salespeople if I had just picked up the phone and asked Cynthia out. But learning the truth now, I was so mad I definitely wouldn't call her. She would have to get her own damn date.

And now I would have to find my own damn job.

A few weeks later, another family friend said he had an advertising connection for me. (I knew I was safe on this one because he had no daughters to ask out.) He had a friend who was office manager for a nice midsized Madison Avenue agency. He couldn't get me a copywriting position but at this point I would take anything in an agency. So a few days later I started work in the mailroom, dutifully delivering packages around Manhattan, distributing mail to the 19th floor and getting coffee for anyone in the agency higher than me...which was everyone.

	REGULAR		OVERTIME			GROSS	DEDUCTIONS				MISCELLANEOUS		NET PAY
PERIOD ENDING	HRS.	AMOUNT	HRS.	AMOUNT		EARNINGS	N.Y.S. WITH. TAX	N.Y.S. DIS. TAX	SOC. SECURITY AND WITH. TAX	BLUE CROSS	CODE	AMOUNT	
SEP 30 60		100.00				100.00	.60	.50	16.30				82.60

LAWRENCE C. GUMBINNER
ADVERTISING AGENCY, INC.
NEW YORK 21, N. Y.

EMPLOYEE'S PAY STATEMENT

My first advertising paycheck...for two weeks in the mailroom.
As my career progressed, I made a little more.

While I was working in the mailroom, I took advantage of every opportunity to learn about the profession I was dipping my toe into. That meant reading as many communications as I could that passed through the mailroom. I worked late many nights not because of a devotion to the job as much as a devotion to not getting caught reading the confidential memos I would be delivering the next day.

As a mailroom guy I seemed to have had some sort of cloak of invisibility that let me hang around often-important confidential meetings hearing crucial strategic discussions without curtailing their candid conversations. And one time I overheard a response that I'll never forget.

A group of senior account executives was meeting to discuss a new campaign our creative people had developed for Tareyton cigarettes. It was our biggest account and so any decisions that were made were crucial to the health of the agency. The senior account person, Stan, liked the new approach and had presented it to the other account people and was soliciting their opinions.

Florence, a senior account executive on other accounts, voiced serious doubts about the new campaign. The Tareyton account executive was really irritated that Florence didn't like the campaign.

"What the hell do you know about cigarettes, Flo? You don't even smoke."

She responded, "I'll bet Norman B. Norman (a well-known ad person) never used a sanitary napkin in his life. But he sure sold a hell of a lot of them with his "Modess because..." ad campaign.

Modess, Shmodess. Eavesdropping on the meeting, I loved both Florence's logic and her guts in standing up to the head of the agency's largest account. It was a valuable lesson to help me in the profession I was about to dive into.

After several months in the mailroom I took a night course in copywriting at New York University and built up a body of homework, skinny though that body was. Then one day, in a burst of courage, when delivering mail to the agency creative director, Bob Marshall, along with his mail I left samples of my work in his in-box. When he called me to his office later that day, I was a nervous wreck. But I listened incredulously as he told me that he wasn't sure but he believed there was a chance that I might have some talent.

A few days later I sat in my own tiny office sharpening pencils waiting for my first assignment as — tah-DAH! — a Junior Copywriter.

* * *

I didn't know it at the time but my graduation from the mailroom was the cue for my memorable people adventures to start. And it took less than a month.

As in any job, when you're low man on the totem pole you get the grunt work to do. Radio was once the king of media. But when television came on the scene, radio took a back seat and radio projects often were shunted down to the junior copywriters…and you couldn't get any more junior than me. And so it was that one of my first assignments was to write a radio commercial for one of our clients, *Redbook Magazine*. The aim was simple: I was given an advance copy of the next issue. I had to choose the story that I thought would stand the best chance of convincing listeners to buy it on the newsstand and then I had to build a commercial around it.

The formula for the commercials was basic. Pull some gee-whiz facts and quotes from the story, and then write sixty seconds' worth of script for an announcer to read. Add some sound effects and music for color and you have it. Not an earthshaking task but I was as excited as if I had been given the assignment of writing a feature film. My first radio spot!

It was the era of John Kennedy and one of the lead pieces in the magazine was about Carolyn Kennedy's life in the White House. I chose it as the subject of my first commercial and began. Unsure of myself, I wrote and re-wrote and then re-wrote again. I proudly made my first expense account purchase, a cheap Radio Shack stopwatch to make sure my script ran exactly sixty seconds, no longer, no less. I timed it, re-timed it, and then re-re-timed it.

I finally worked up the courage to show this, my first copywriting effort, to the creative director. To make sure it was the right length, besides timing the spot, I had counted the words— exactly 83. And, according to him, I had gotten most of them

One of my first copywriting assignments was to write a radio commercial selling this magazine. I used this article to attract the listeners' attention.

wrong. He didn't like my commercial very much. My choice of subject was okay, he said, but my execution was boring.

"If someone heard this on their car radio while they were driving," he told me with his clipped British accent, "there was a real danger they'd fall asleep at the wheel."

But he knew this was my first try and was encouraging. He gave me great advice like, "Stop them in the first eight seconds or they'll never hear the rest of what you have to say," and "Write conversationally...like you're talking to people, not writing to them." I was to carry these and other bits of wisdom with me for the rest of my writing career. It was simple stuff but to a novice copywriter it was as if his words came down from the mountain engraved in stone.

I went back to my office armed with his precious advice and started from scratch. Again. It took me two days of writing and rewriting and re-rewriting before I had a script to show him and then another half day to get up the courage to show it.

Amazingly, he liked it. He, of course made a series of changes but when I brought him the re-re-revised script he smiled and okayed it for showing to our *Redbook* client.

I was too junior to go to client meetings so, while the account executive presented my firstborn to the client, I paced back and forth in my office, chain-smoking the Tareyton cigarettes provided free of charge by our American Tobacco client.

A year later (or so it seemed) my phone rang. It was the account exec. The client had bought my commercial. It was okay to produce!

As a junior, I had no say in the casting of the announcer. That was the job of the agency producers who oversaw the production of all the radio and television commercials. The producer on the *Redbook* account, Mort Kasman, called me with the date, time and place of the recording session.

The night before the session, I managed only about one hour of sleep. We took a cab to the studio for the 2 o'clock appointment and arrived several minutes early. But the announcer was nowhere to be seen. After ten minutes, Mort called the announcer's agent who confirmed that the announcer knew about the session but the agent had no idea why he wasn't at the studio.

Ten minutes later in walked the announcer. He and Mort were old friends and, despite the lateness, they shook hands warmly. He introduced himself to me and, as he shook my hand, he apologized profusely. His apology carried with it a sincerity I could feel as well as a familiar fragrance I could smell...alcohol.

He looked at me and smiled. "I know what you're thinking," he laughed. "But don't worry. I'll give you a great spot. You have to understand," he continued, "I just signed a contract today that's going to make me a millionaire and I had to celebrate a bit. I'll tell you about it after we finish."

We went into the studio and, true to his word, he delivered the spot like a pro, bringing my words to life beautifully. After just a few takes, we had it and, as the engineer began editing sound effects and music into the spot, the announcer explained what had happened.

He really had reason to celebrate. That morning he had signed a contract to be the announcer on a new late night television show that was debuting soon. The host of that show was Johnny Carson. Johnny's announcer—and mine that day—was Ed McMahon.

He was right. In the years that followed, he gained fame and popularity as Carson's sidekick and that, along with lucrative work as spokesman for Publisher's Clearing House and several other major advertisers, made him those millions he talked about that day in the studio. But, unhappily, he was better with a microphone than he was with money and when he passed away in 2009 he was heavily in debt.

But it was a great moment for me to meet him that day in the studio as his career was about to launch into the stratosphere.

* * *

One day while I was distributing mail, one of our art directors asked me if I'd like to model for an ad for our client, Noilly Prat vermouth. I was flattered...until I saw the ad. I had nothing to be flattered about. This was the launch of my modeling career. And the end of it.

* * *

As I gained experience and grew in seniority, I had more to say about the casting of my commercials. I found that it's one of the most important and, often the most difficult, parts of producing a television spot. The right actor in the right part can make a spot.

On the other hand, the wrong one can live with you forever,

grinding you in the eyeballs every time your spot appears.

Because of this, I became demanding during casting. And it was because I was particularly stubborn about casting one part that I met an idol of mine and, although the circumstances were bittersweet, I enjoyed a moment that was electric. And unforgettable.

The commercial was to take place on a boat to be shot in Los Angeles. Before we flew to L.A., we had sent the casting director the storyboard illustrating the flow of the commercial and described who we were looking for. The heart of the spot was the ship's captain and at our first meeting she showed us a videotape of the men she had auditioned before we arrived. They all were clichéd ship captains—captain's cap, squinty eyes and a pipe gripped firmly in their teeth. It was admittedly a safe way to go but I didn't want Popeye. I was looking for someone offbeat and more interesting.

Two days of casting sessions produced no one we liked and a crisis was developing. We were scheduled to shoot on Monday and union rules stated that if we didn't cancel the shoot by noon Friday, we would have to pay the film crew anyway, a $15,000 client-upsetting proposition. And if we delayed the shoot another day or two, it would be almost impossible to finish the commercial in time for its first air date, something our already-difficult client would not enjoy at all.

On Friday morning, a parade of hopefuls produced more Popeye lookalikes. There was no one captain that would satisfy me. I had compromised before and had hated myself afterwards. Not this time.

But the clock was ticking and as 11 o'clock passed, panic started to set in. Then, at 11:15 magic happened. The door opened and in walked one of my movie idols—Lon Chaney, Jr. His most famous role was as the Wolfman in the Frankenstein series and when I was a child, accidentally seeing even just a few seconds of his Wolfman in a preview would drive me to sleep with my parents for days.

Lon Chaney as the Wolfman had cost me many hours of sleep when I was a kid. When he came in years later (without the makeup) on a casting call for Edge Shave Gel it occurred to me that with his fame as a werewolf it would be pretty ironic to hire him to do a commercial for a shaving product.

Although I would never admit it to any of my fellow ten-year-olds, his bear-like, dull-witted Lenny in the film *Of Mice and Men* had moved me to tears.

But the man before us had aged. Chaney wore slippers on his swollen feet, squinted through thick glasses and spoke hoarsely. It was apparent that he really wanted the work, even needed it. He had studied the script in the waiting room before he came in but it had not done any good. His first reading was stilted and he knew it.

"I've always been terrible at cold readings," he apologized.

I always discounted an actor's bad first reading, chalking it up to nervousness, and always gave them a second one automatically.

But his second one was no better. The director, sneaking a glance at his watch, was about to thank Chaney and politely dismiss him when I interrupted. I offered Chaney some direction for a third reading. I could feel the daggers piercing me from my team but to hell with it. He had earned a last chance just because of who he was...or had been.

But, alas, there was no change. We thanked him and offered him a glass of water before he went back out into the 90-degree Los Angeles summer. He took it and, to everyone's dismay—and my delight—sat down and started to sip it. To hell with the time, I thought. This was a moment.

With a little prodding from me, Chaney started spinning tales about his glory days in Hollywood. He told us how they had shot his very first transformation from the hapless Larry Talbot to the Wolfman: his head lay cradled in a wooden frame as they added hair to his face little by little and shot the changes one frame at a time....for eleven nonstop hours.

And he smiled proudly when he told how his dog really saved the wizened old gypsy actress, Maria Ouspenskaya, from being crushed when the gypsy wagon she was sitting in started overturning on a muddy sound stage.

Realizing I had pushed my group—and the clock—as far as I could, I offered my hand to Chaney to help him up. On the way out, I gave the traditional casting person's turndown speech, "We'll be in touch with your agent." Then, with emotion, I added something that thrills me to this day.

"Mr. Chaney, I was very little when I saw *Of Mice and Men* and your Lenny was so good that it made me cry." It was true and the tears that welled up in his eyes told me that he knew it. He glowed as he made one of his last exits. He was to die that year.

Now the clock read 11:50. Ten minutes to cancel or else. As

the director picked up the phone to cancel the Monday shoot, the door opened and a last-minute candidate stuck his head in.

"How ya doin'? Ya think I'm too late?" he asked in a voice rich with a familiar accent. A fellow expatriate Brooklynite.

"Not at all," I lied. "Just read your part quickly."

I liked his rugged, real-person look and the accent worked for me. Halfway through his first read-through, the director and I looked at each other and smiled. He was perfect. He had the job and we had our captain...and our Monday shoot.

He turned out to be a great choice. Vic Tayback was wonderful to work with and equally good in the part. I wasn't surprised a few years later when he became a major television star playing Mel, the owner of the diner in the TV sitcom, "Alice".

And to this day, I still believe that had we not treated the aging Lon Chaney as we had that day, Fate wouldn't have thanked us by giving us Vic Tayback at the 11th hour.

* * *

Sometimes we advertising folk can become minor celebrities in our own right. When I had moved to Los Angeles to join BBDO/West, one ad campaign my group had created gave us a measure of fame that led to my meeting an incredibly outrageous person.

Some people from my creative department told me about a great restaurant in a hotel they had all visited a week earlier. The food was good, but the real reason for going was the maître d', Richard, who all by himself, they said, was worth a visit to the restaurant.

At the time, our ad campaign for our Western Airlines client promoted the extra legspace Western offered. "You Get Three Feet for Your Two Legs" was running throughout the western U.S. in a heavy TV and radio schedule. The centerpiece of the campaign was a marvelous upbeat jingle written by Perry Botkin, Jr. During the group's first visit to the restaurant, Richard had learned that they were responsible for the campaign and the jingle. He loved it and had made a funny fuss about it. My people assured me that it would be fun to go there.

A few nights later, as we entered, Richard saw us and instantly remembered the group. Without a moment's hesitation—or an iota of self-consciousness—he climbed on a chair and banged a spoon on a metal tray.

"Ladies and gentlemen," he announced, "we have celebrities here. These people are responsible for the Western Airlines jingle, 'You Get Three Feet For Your Two Legs.' To welcome them, let's everybody sing!"

And with that, spoon in hand, he led the entire restaurant, staid Beverly Hills-ites and all, in a rousing rendition of our jingle as he marched us through the restaurant to our table, his spoon now a drum major's baton.

Throughout the meal he was just as funny, uninhibited and outrageous. His recitation of the evening's specials included an unforgettable quasi-Shakespearean description: "The baby shrimp are so fresh they have been ripped untimely from their mother's womb." As promised, he was worth the price of the whole meal.

I visited the restaurant several times after that and once even scored significant points with a new girlfriend by being recognized by Richard as we entered. But not long after, I returned to find Richard was gone. Somehow, the place just wasn't the same.

A few years later, I was in a doctor's office browsing through tattered back issues of *People Magazine* when I saw a profile of Richard. But he wasn't a maître d' anymore. Through his wit and warmth, he had risen to become famous not as a person who helped people eat but as one who helped them not eat. In the article, I discovered that Richard's last name was Simmons.

* * *

I occasionally used the creative freedom I had to develop advertising that would take me to interesting places to shoot. And once I helped create a campaign that helped me meet some very interesting people.

At BBDO/West we hads recommended to a client who manufactured computer peripherals that they run an "image" campaign. Often a purchase is made on the basis of not just the consumer's judgment of the product but of how they feel about the company that makes it. While our client's products were very good, the company itself was not well known and so didn't inspire confidence. Because of this, it was difficult for anyone to recommend our client's products to their superiors. To remedy this, we recommended to the client that they run an ad campaign that would make the company appear big and prosperous.

Our campaign called for ads that were short essays about the future of computing. What would make the ads unique was that they would be written by well-known futurists—respected visionaries who had insights into tomorrow. The ads would say nothing about our client or its products. We believed that these thoughtful essays by famous authors appearing above our client's logo would give an impression of importance to the company.

I've been a science fiction fan since I was a young boy and one of my favorite authors of all time was Ray Bradbury. As a boy, I had sat in the public library for hours reading his books like *Martian Chronicles* and *The Illustrated Man*. With his prestige and talent, he'd be perfect as a contributor. Besides, he lived in Los Angeles so I might have a chance to meet him.

We contacted his agent, the deal was made very easily and it was agreed I would talk to him by phone. He was everything I could ever hope for in a literary idol—witty, gracious, and, above all, enthusiastic. Heaven knows, he certainly didn't need the money. When I told him the subject we wanted him to write about— computers in the future—he was excited. This was in the late '70's and the computer revolution that would be started by Apple with its Macintosh was still some five years in the future. We discussed the fact that there was a vague, but growing, awareness of these machines called computers and that there were many people who were afraid that they might displace humans. Bradbury decided to write a piece that would reassure people that there was nothing to fear from them.

The piece was excellent—brief, as requested, and witty as expected. But it was a bit longer than the ad space allowed. So I had to gather up every last ounce of nerve to cut his essay slightly. Me, Donny Spector from Brooklyn, editing Ray Bradbury. Chutzpah incarnate, I thought. But it was necessary so I did it.

When I sent him my edits, he was fine about them, made one or two suggestions and the ad copy was set. Now came the best part— photographing him for the ad. We set up a date and time for the photo session. I would meet him at the photographer's studio and would finally get to meet my idol.

He was just as gracious in person as he was on the phone. I generally enjoy photo sessions because I like to talk to the subjects to relax them and reduce any camera-consciousness.

Bradbury was relaxed and naturally animated before the camera so I had little to do but enjoy myself. After a half hour, the photographer announced that he was happy. He had his shot somewhere in the dozen rolls of film he had exposed.

The next day we got the photos from the studio and we had a number of good portraits of Bradbury to choose from. One group of shots was particularly animated and we chose the one we would use in the ad from among those. Then I remembered what we had been discussing when we got that particularly animated shot.. It was slightly less esoteric than Computers In Our Future—we had been talking about a then-popular porn star, Linda Lovelace.

The ad I created that let me meet one of my idols.

* * *

While doing this series, I had a chance to talk to another of my favorite sci fi authors, Isaac Asimov. Because he was in New York and I was in Los Angeles, we had a long distance telephone relationship. Asimov was very nice but more businesslike than Bradbury so when it came to editing his essay, I chickened out and sent him my suggested changes by mail rather than discussing them by phone. But he was professional about it and accepted them without question.

Shortly after the ad appeared, I got a request from the head of my BBDO/West office. He was an officer in an organization that wanted to have Asimov as a guest speaker. He thought that, because of my relationship with the author, I would have a better chance of getting him to accept the offer.

I called Asimov in New York and asked him if he would speak before the group. Not possible, he told me in no uncertain terms. I assured him that his fee was no object and they were flexible about the date of the meeting and would be happy to arrange it around his schedule. That wasn't the problem, he explained. He was about to sail to Europe on the QE2 for five days to attend a three-hour meeting in Paris, then turn around the next day and sail back.

The reason for spending nearly two weeks on the water for a three-hour meeting? One of the world's greatest authors of science fiction and science fact, a man whose worlds of fiction were filled with intergalactic rocket ships and space cruisers, admitted to me that he was afraid of flying.

* * *

Even when I was very senior at major agencies, I would have given it all up in a heartbeat if the phone rang and someone had said, "Let's take a lunch...I have this feature I'd like you to direct." Though my career had always been centered around writing, my true love had always been directing film.

And it was a directing gig that led me to work with one of the most genuinely nice celebrities I've ever met.

While I was in New York, I had actually studied acting for three years just to better understand how an actor thinks. I felt it would help me direct actors better. But my advertising career had taken precedence and by 1980 I had directed only one short film and a half dozen commercials. The film had actually done well, winning several awards in film festivals around the world and one of the commercials had been a finalist in the Clio Awards, a prestigious TV commercial competition. But it still wasn't enough to move me into full-time directing.

Then fate stepped in. A commercial producer I had worked with had gotten a contract to produce a business film on the subject of employee theft. He asked me if I would write it. I would, I answered, if I could also direct it. It was a deal, he said.

Employees stealing from their companies were costing American businesses over $10 billion a year. The finished film would be sold to companies concerned about employee theft and would be shown to their employees to dissuade them from stealing. I spent weeks researching the subject in libraries, reading books and newspaper archives. Then I went out into the field and interviewed over a dozen people including uniformed police, detectives, FBI agents and security directors of major corporations. I even was introduced to, and interviewed, some convicted thieves.

Eventually, I distilled over a month of research into a twenty-minute script, *The Ten Billion Dollar Ripoff*, and, after the inevitable revisions, the company that was underwriting the project signed off on it. And so we began production.

The number one order of business was casting the spokesperson. Rather than using the threat of getting caught to deter employees from stealing from their employer, I had chosen to use positive persuasion as my method of convincing my audience to be honest.

Because of this, the spokesperson was key to the pitch. Should he or she be a strong and parental authority figure? Or should they be likable—"one of the guys" who the audience could identify with? I had gone through over a dozen possible spokespersons when my producer made a suggestion. He was friends with Casey Kasem's agent and thought that Casey might be interested in doing the film.

Kasem's *American Top 40* music countdown had been on the top of the radio charts for years and when I spoke to him on the phone he sounded friendly enough. But a disk jockey as a spokesman? I frankly doubted it but, out of courtesy, I agreed to meet with him.

He came to my office and in less than fifteen minutes I knew Casey was my man. He was as likable in person as his radio persona. And happily, he was a good actor—he had video clips of some guest spots he had done on several dramatic TV shows and a very funny impression of the actor Peter Falk he had done at a Friar's Club roast. He was eager to do my film.

Money certainly wasn't his motivation. His Top 40 radio show was, at the time, the most widely distributed syndicated radio show in the world. He was constantly doing lucrative voiceovers for TV commercials. He had a contract to be the voice of NBC television in all their promotions. And he did a number of voices for Saturday morning cartoon characters, incredibly lucrative work thanks to union rules on pay scales and residuals.

But what Casey really wanted to do was on-camera acting…a clear case of the grass is always greener. And that was something I could certainly identify with. He was a successful radio personality who wanted to act; I was a successful ad executive who wanted to direct. He liked my script and we liked each other. We shook on it.

The production schedule called for five days of shooting, three in various locations around Los Angeles and two on a big sound stage in Hollywood. That's where Casey would do his part. The stage was the single most expensive part of the production budget, largely because of my vision of what I wanted the on-camera spokesman portion of the film to look like. I envisioned an all-black set with Casey appearing in isolated islands of light. But my concept didn't come cheap. Besides the rental fee for the two days of shooting, we had to pay an extra day's rental before the shoot to paint the stage black and then another the day after the shoot to paint it back to the white we found it in. And that didn't even include paying the crew to paint it.

After three days of location shooting, we moved to the stage. That's when I discovered my black stage was costly in another way. When we looked at Casey through the camera, his dark hair kept getting lost against the dark background so we had to adjust the lights to separate his hair from the background. And each time we moved the camera, we had to re-adjust the lights. As on many shoots, I found that lighting took longer than I had planned.

I had also chosen to save several hundred dollars by not renting a teleprompter with the script on it. Mistake! Retakes of a scene when an actor forgets his lines add up. The added cost of the teleprompter would have been nothing compared to the money it would have saved by speeding up production. The result was that the shoot on the stage was going slowly. We were rapidly falling behind schedule.

In the midst of all the pressure the bright spot was Casey. He was calm, unflappable and friendly. And, most important for the film, my impression of him during his interview was right—he was a good actor who took direction well. He was delivering a very sincere, believable performance, just what I had envisioned.

But by the middle of the second day, it looked like I would only be able to shoot two-thirds of that fine performance. It seemed more and more doubtful that I would finish in time. And the budget couldn't afford another day's stage rental.

Then, during a production break I had called, a miracle happened. I was standing outside, trying to come up with an alternative plan if I didn't finish shooting Casey that day. My best bet was to shoot as much of him as I could and then rewrite the script, changing the portion of him that I wouldn't have time to shoot to Casey speaking voice-over—his voice off-camera over other footage I had shot. It would weaken the film but it seemed the only way...until I felt a hand on my shoulder. It was Casey.

"Are we going to finish in time?" he asked.

"I think there's a chance," I lied unconvincingly.

But Casey knew the truth and, after a pause, said, "I really like the film and I think its moral message of honesty is important."

That made me feel better. But where was he was going?

"I want to make sure you finish this film properly," he continued, "so I want you to keep as much of my fee as it takes to rent this stage for another day."

I was stunned. But that Kasem smile was real. He meant it. He was willing to pay for the stage so we could finish. I was overcome with emotion and didn't say anything for a while.

"I couldn't do that, Casey." But he insisted. I thanked him and told him I'd think about it.

I called my executive producer who was as startled as I was. He had many years of high level experience on shows like *The Hallmark Hall of Fame* and had regularly dealt with star talent. He had never heard of anything like this. But we both agreed we couldn't let Casey pay for it. Instead, the producer went back to the company underwriting the film. They were pleased with my early footage and so they agreed to pay for the additional day of stage rental.

Their investment paid off. *The Ten Billion Dollar Ripoff* turned out to be a great success. Films like this that were targeted to sell

In directing Casey Kasem in my film I found him to be natural and believable. His performance was a big element in the film's success.

to businesses generally make back their investment in 18-24 months. *Ripoff* went into the black in only eleven months. And it went on to win a major award at the New York International Film Festival.

I lost touch with Casey after we finished the film but some thirty years later I came across his email address and wrote to him. I recapped the success the film had enjoyed and thanked him again for the incredibly generous offer he had made. After thirty years I wasn't sure he'd remember the film or me. But he most certainly did.

He replied in his gracious manner:

"Thank you, Don, for all the kind words. I do remember that day! And I still believe that it was one of the most important projects that I have ever worked on and believe that it should have been shown in every school. You're too kind! Thank you for the trip down memory lane! Best, Casey."

All the money and awards notwithstanding, the high point of the whole experience for me was that moment outside the sound stage when I had that quiet conversation with a genuinely nice guy.

Three years later, Casey passed away. When I learned that, I cried.

* * *

Not all my movie heroes have been on the screen. Some have been behind the camera. And one day I had a chance to meet one of them.

Frank Capra had directed some of my favorite films like *It's a Wonderful Life* and *Mr. Smith Goes to Washington*, both starring Jimmy Stewart. His movies often were so unashamedly corny that critics and audiences fondly dubbed his style "Capracorn." But as a sucker for the corny, I loved them and admired the man. When I started working on a project, little did I know that it would lead me to meet him.

My client, Sunrise Company, was a builder of country club communities in the Palm Springs area. When they told us that they would be developing homes for a new project to be named PGA West in the village of La Quinta, we knew we faced a problem. As lovely as La Quinta was, it was virtually unknown compared to its well-known desert resort neighbors, Palm Springs and Palm Desert. Asking people to purchase expensive condos in a little-known area like La Quinta would be difficult. So we knew that our first priority would be to raise La Quinta's profile.

While I was in the process of doing research on La Quinta I learned that Capra had been the honorary mayor of La Quinta for many years. He still lived there and, through some friends, I was able to contact him and set up a meeting.

He was a delight. In his eighties, he was energetic, friendly and funny. I could see why actors and actresses had loved working with him. I asked him about his experience with La Quinta.

He told me that in the mid 1930's he was filming *Lost Horizon* in the mountains that bordered the desert area east of Los Angeles.

When they finished shooting for the day, instead of going to the busier Palm Springs, he and his actors preferred to retire to La Quinta to eat, drink and gamble. The many stars who, over the years, enjoyed La Quinta with him included Ronald Coleman, Jane Wyatt and Jimmy Stewart.

The ad that gave an almost-forgotten town new life...
and my career a bit of a boost.

Capra was great company and I stretched out our meeting as long as I could. When I knew I couldn't prolong our chat any longer, I thanked him and reluctantly said goodbye.

If meeting him was all that I got out of my research I would have been happy. But, using one thing he told me, I developed an ad that helped launch a new popularity for the little-known town.

One of the actors, Capra said, who enjoyed visiting La Quinta was Clark Gable. The ad I did featured a picture of him dressed as

Rhett Butler in *Gone with the Wind* with a headline based on one of the most famous lines ever uttered in a movie.

The ad got a lot of attention and, more important, it helped set PGA West on the road to the great success it enjoyed as the Western Home of American Golf. And I owe a share of the credit to my all-too-brief friendship with Frank Capra.

* * *

One of my most memorable moments in the business was the time I met Porky Pig and Bugs Bunny and Elmer Fudd and Tweety Bird and Daffy Duck. As a kid I had enjoyed the characters from Warner Brothers' *Looney Tunes* cartoons but never knew who gave them voices. The father of all those voices was Mel Blanc. It was the same Mel Blanc who played multiple characters on the Jack Benny radio show I had listened to religiously every Sunday.

One of my favorite characters on the show was his very nasal Mexican peasant with a vocabulary limited to single syllable words. An example:

Jack: What's your name?

Mel: Sy.

Jack: Sy?

Mel: Si.

Jack: What's your sister's name?

Mel: Sue.

Jack: Sue?

Mel: Si.

It was only after listening to the show for years that I learned that, besides the many characters he did, Mel also voiced the sound of the hard-starting engine of Jack's antique car, the Maxwell. I never understood why the studio audience always laughed uproariously whenever Jack tried to start his car until I learned that they were enjoying Mel doing all the car's hacking, coughing and backfiring with nothing but his mouth and vocal chords.

And then one day Mel stood before me in a Hollywood recording studio. One of the most popular commercial series I worked on was a cartoon series for Western Airlines and the script that day called for the voice of a small bird. Without my knowing it, my producer had cast Mel for the part. I was dazzled.

Tight production schedule or not, there was no way I would pass up a chance to talk to him. So while the other voices, the producer and the engineer stood by, I chatted with him.

I asked him about the legal status of his *Looney Tunes* characters' voices. Could he do Bugs or Elmer or Porky if asked? Mel explained that he was free to do the voices since he had created them. But the actual phrases like Bugs' "What's up doc?" and Porky's "Tha-tha-that's all folks!" were owned by Warner Brothers and couldn't be spoken by the character voices. But, Mel smiled, he would never, ever do the voices even without their signature lines.

"Warner Brothers has been so good to me over the years," he explained, "that I would never do that to them no matter how much money I was offered." You could feel his sincerity and I was impressed.

We proceeded with the recording session and it went beautifully. Mel not only created a funny voice for his character, he ad libbed a few small changes that made his character—and the commercial—more memorable.

Just before he left I had one more question to ask him and it was a very important one to me. Jack Benny had been one of my idols. He had passed away several years earlier and I asked Mel if he was as nice as he appeared to be on the radio.

"No he wasn't," Mel replied.

I was crushed until a moment later Mel added, "He was even

nicer. Jack was one of the nicest, kindest people I've ever known."

And to me, that generous, caring statement put Mel in the same class as Jack Benny.

∞ 3 ∞

THE TRUTH ABOUT TRUTH IN ADVERTISING.

The American public has always had an uneasy, suspicious relationship with anyone who tries to sell them something. So it's only natural that those feelings of quasi-paranoia have draped themselves over the advertising industry. Popular books and movies like *The Hucksters* and *The Man in the Grey Flannel Suit* didn't help, portraying advertising people as slick, do-anything-for-a-buck used car salesmen.

Then, in the mid-1960s, the public's worst suspicions about advertising were realized in two celebrated cases.

One technique for demonstrating how well a product works is known as the "torture test." The strategy is simple: give the product much tougher use than it would actually receive. If it can survive the supertough test, the reasoning goes, it can certainly do its normal job.

The classic example of that was a campaign for Timex watches, "It takes a licking and keeps on ticking." In one commercial, the spokesman strapped a Timex to the propeller of an outboard motor and revved it up. They then cut the motor, untaped the watch and zoomed in for a tight close-up to show the second hand still twirling merrily around. Convincing and strictly legitimate.

Another TV torture test showed how well a shaving cream worked. "So good it can shave sandpaper," the announcer claimed.

And, sure enough, there was the razor shaving a clean-cut swath through the foam leaving nothing but smooth paper behind it. It was convincing as hell. And fraudulent as hell. It was revealed that there was a difference between this sandpaper and the kind you buy at the hardware store: this sand wasn't glued to the paper. Shave it off? You could have blown it off. The ad agency and people involved were found guilty of fraud and paid heavy fines. And the credibility of advertising took a nosedive.

In another TV spot, the camera, sitting in the passenger seat of a car, showed the passing scenery through the curved windshield to show just how distortion-free the advertiser's glass was. The trouble was that the windshield was not only free of distortion...it was revealed that it was also free of glass. And once again the advertising industry took a big hit.

Some misadventures didn't make the papers...or the courtroom. One famous spot demonstrated the toughness of a pickup truck by having a parachute drag it out of the back of a cargo plane flying ten feet over a hard-surfaced runway. The truck hit the runway hard and as soon as it did, actors ran up to it, unhooked it from the pallet it was strapped to and drove it off into the sunset. That was some tough truck, eh?

This one may have been but the first two they used weren't. When they hit the runway they were bent so badly they were undriveable. A friend of mine who was on the shoot told me they were considering giving up on the demo when they got lucky on the third try. Legally the spot may have been legitimate—the truck shown had really survived the drop. But the ethics of implying a 100% success rate when it was actually 33% were questionable.

* * *

In my years in the business both before and since these episodes, I was never involved, nor was I ever asked to be involved, in any kind of misrepresentation. And I honestly believe these kinds of things were relatively infrequent. But, rare though they may have been, they confirmed the public's very worst fears and the Federal Trade Commission, along with Congress and the courts, came down hard on the industry. One of the results was that ultra-strict rules were laid down concerning product demonstrations in TV spots. Precise records had to be kept on how a demonstration was shot. Misrepresenting reality in any way had to be avoided.

If, for example, your commercial was showing a side-by-side demonstration of how your laundry detergent cleaned better than a competitor's, you had to have the same kind and quantity of dirt or stain on absolutely identical fabrics, use the same pre-wash for the same period of time, wash both products in the same kind of washing machine using the same water temperature and the same wash cycles. Both fabrics had to be treated identically before they were filmed; one couldn't be ironed and not the other.

The days of "trust me" were gone. Affidavits had to be signed by everyone involved in the commercial testifying to the legitimacy of the demo. The affidavits were legally admissible in court if the demo was ever called into question and penalties could be severe, up to jail time. And they could be exacted on anyone involved with the commercial from the director all the way down to the prop person.

Those word-filled screens at the end of car commercials that look like the bottom line of an eye chart? They were born during this era as a reaction to abuses. For a long time, for instance, bait-and-switching was fairly common. A low-ball price was quoted in the commercial. But show up at the dealer and they had "just sold" the last of that low-priced model. But they just happened to have a model for just a few more dollars.....!

"Enough," said the FCC. There had to be full disclosure or no disclosure. Any time a price was mentioned in a car spot, all the conditions, restrictions, and qualifiers that could affect that price had to be shown.

The type on that final screen you see may be tiny but it represents a very big stick for consumers. It's there to prevent false, or even honest but overly-aggressive, advertising claims from being made. And it gives car-buying consumers who feel they've been misled legal grounds on which to base their claims.

But the enforcement of many of the fraud-prevention measures isn't always easy. The dividing line between producing a commercial fraudulently and simply using production shortcuts to save time and money isn't always clear-cut. There are often good reasons for playing around with reality when you're filming a commercial.

For instance, since time immemorial, an important moment in a beer commercial has been the pour shot—the golden liquid cascading into the glass being crowned by a rich, white foamy head. Problem: the head and heat can't coexist. The heat from the studio lights can cause the foam to collapse prematurely making filming a beautiful head very difficult.

But there's a simple solution: put a thin film of soap around the rim of the glass and, thanks to some arcane law of the natural universe, the head holds up longer under the lights. This wasn't done to mislead the public. After all, beer does have a head and it isn't normally drunk under hot studio lights. It was done to save production time and money. But in the wake of the clampdown, even this harmless practice was frowned on.

* * *

In another celebrated case, the New York office of my own agency, BBDO, came under fire for a Campbell's Vegetable Soup spot. Understandably, they wanted to show the vegetables in the soup. But they came up against a basic law of physics: vegetables don't float.

Without the vegetables showing, the soup shot was incredibly boring. So, in order to make the celery, peas and carrots more visible, they placed marbles in the soup. The marbles dropped to the bottom of the bowl, displacing the vegetables and forcing them to the top. Not a problem, everyone said. After all, everyone knows there really are vegetables in vegetable soup.

But, although it didn't occur to anyone at the time, they had created a problem. With the vegetables showing on top, some people could interpret it to mean that the soup contained vegetables from top to bottom—more than it actually did. That hadn't been the reason for using the marbles but it was the unintentional result. The agency and client were fined for the misstep and, as it had across the industry, production paranoia marched on.

When I moved to Needham, Harper & Steers Advertising in New York, I found this paranoia was almost tangible. The agency was in trouble because of a commercial they had created for their client, Sucrets throat lozenges. To illustrate the effectiveness of Sucrets graphically, they showed a man with an animated fire burning in his throat. The announcer promised that Sucrets "Puts out the fire in your throat." The lozenge went in, the cartoon fire went out and the sufferer smiled. All fairly standard use of symbolism to sell over-the-counter drug products like Sucrets.

Despite the agency's position that this was just a harmless graphic device to help viewers remember the spot, the Federal Trade Commission took issue with the claim, maintaining it was an overstatement of the product's effectiveness. They fined the agency and put it, and the people involved, on probation. Any kind of violation concerning not just Sucrets but any of the agency's other clients could lead to further substantial fines for the agency and possibly even jail sentences for the anyone connected with the account that was deemed in violation.

This had a direct effect on me. Soon after I arrived at Needham, I was asked to create a package of Sucrets commercials. My group developed storyboards for a half dozen thirty-second spots and my creative director approved them. But before I could show the storyboards to the client, they had to be reviewed by our agency attorney. It was an unforgettably painful day, a quintessential exercise in the art of Covering Your Ass.

The attorney and I sat in my office and went over every word in every hand-drawn frame of each storyboard—generally ten to twelve frames to a board—trying to consider every possible interpretation both reasonable and unreasonable, rational and nutso. It took three unholy hours to FTC-proof the storyboards and, by the time we finished, I felt that if some day I did have to go to prison for the commercials, I could at least take a three-hour credit off my sentence.

* * *

In its regulatory exuberance during the '60s and '70s, the FTC often overstepped its bounds, acting as judge, jury and executioner all at the same time. I witnessed one such case from a front row seat.

Bristol-Myers was in a dispute with the FTC based on a new product they had just introduced, Excedrin PM. The government agency believed that extensive testing was required before the product could be released to the public. Bristol-Myers disagreed. Excedrin PM, they maintained, was simply their standard Excedrin with antihistamines added. One of the side effects of antihistamines was drowsiness, so Excedrin PM could be used by headache sufferers to help them sleep. Since both Excedrin and the antihistamine were each approved for use and deemed safe, Bristol-Myers maintained that the product did not require the years of costly testing necessary for a new medication. The FTC disagreed and Bristol-Myers was preparing for a legal battle. But, unknown to Bristol-Myers, the principle battle was not to be fought in the court but in the press.

I was in a meeting in the Bristol-Myers offices on a different product when my client got a terrifying phone call. Accompanied by television cameras, photographers and reporters, FTC agents had raided a drugstore and confiscated the Excedrin PM. My clients were stunned. They knew that pictures of government agents ripping their product from the shelves would give the impression that the FTC had found Excedrin PM unsafe...which was not true. The subtleties of the legal disagreement regarding testing would be lost on the public. The FTC would be heroes—modern-day good guys saving the public from the bad guys of Bristol-Myers. The FTC had done their damage, all without a minute spent in court. Due process had flown out the window. Or, more accurately, it had been thrown out.

The newspapers and TV news programs predictably reported that Excedrin PM had been pulled from store shelves. People who didn't read the rest of the article automatically assumed the product was unsafe. By the time the actual case was adjudicated in favor of Bristol-Myers, the company had lost millions in sales and had to fight an uphill battle to re-establish the product's name and image in the public's mind. It was a classic case of overzealous use—or abuse—of government power.

* * *

The strict new laws gave me an Excedrin-sized headache once when we were shooting a commercial for a new shave product from S.C. Johnson, Edge. Because, instead of a foam, Edge comes from the can in the form of a gel, it offers a number of advantages. One of them, its extra lubricating qualities, makes nicks and cuts rarer than using foam shaves. Not impossible, but less likely.

To promise that, the most important part of the commercial

would be the actor shaving and the shot of the clean-cut result. But with the new stricter rules in effect, we couldn't fake it. The money shot at the end of the spot with the clean-shaven actor would have to be the result of his shaving with Edge by himself. No special treatment, no special cut-covering makeup. The truth-in-advertising affidavits we all would have to sign would have to attest to that. If he cut himself, we would have to wait several days to let him heal, regrow his beard and then shave again...at an overbudget cost of thousands of dollars for cast and crew, stage, etc. If, on the other hand, it was a good shave, we would be able to shoot the cut-free beauty shot and sign affidavits in good conscience.

The auditions gave us fits. We put out a casting call for men in their late twenties with instructions for them to come in with two days' growth of beard. If we liked an actor's look, we would ask him to shave with Edge for us. At the casting session, all went fine until the fourth shaver. He was good-looking and confident, eager to show us how well—and fast—he could shave. He lathered up and, hardly looking in the mirror, started shaving with bold, broad strokes.

By the fifth stroke, his blood was flowing like wine. We yelled for him to stop but his adrenaline was pumping as fast as his blood and he couldn't. By the time he finished, his face looked like he had just met up with the Three Musketeers in a dark alley. We gave him a box of Band-Aids, thanked him with straight faces and, when he left the room, collapsed in helpless laughter.

But the joke could be on us. What if that happened when we were really shooting?

We cast another less swashbuckling actor and on the day of the shoot, all went smoothly. But no matter how satisfied we were with the introductory scenes we were getting, the shave at the end of the day loomed. When we had shot all the scenes of our bearded actor, the moment arrived. We would now film him starting to shave, then would stop the camera and let him finish up without the pressure of lights, camera and crew hanging over him.

He lathered up and we all held our collective breath. At the director's call of "Action!" he began the Big Shave. Stroke. Stroke. Rinse blade. Stroke. Stroke. No blood. Stroke. Stroke. Rinse blade. Stroke. Still no blood.

"Cut!" cried the director.

"Don't use that word," I cried back.

Time for our actor to finish the shave off-camera. No lights or crew. Just four nervous ad agency guys staring at him from three feet away. The director made a suggestion…"Why don't you guys get the hell out of here?"

We took his suggestion and stepped out of the studio into the warm summer afternoon. But after a minute, we couldn't stand the anxious waiting. As I opened the door, I heard the director's loud voice crying, "Oh, shit!"

I broke into a run. Disaster. As I turned the corner, I saw them—the now clean-shaven actor and the director standing there with big grins on their faces. And two big middle fingers pointing up in the air. The shave—and our affidavits—had turned out just fine.

* * *

Health claims and cigarettes don't quite go together…except once early in my career.

One of the first products I wrote for was Dual Filter Tareyton cigarettes from American Tobacco Company. In those days, smoking didn't carry the social and medical stigma—and the advertising prohibitions—that it has today. So I leapt happily into every job I was given, especially since I was a two-pack-a-day smoker myself and got all the Tareytons I could suck on absolutely free of charge.

One day, a unique creative assignment came through. Our media department had bought time on a Navajo radio station in New Mexico and I was asked to write a series of Tareyton radio spots for it. Since I knew nothing about the Navajo people and what would appeal to them, I got the name of the radio personality who would be reading my spots and called him in New Mexico.

A Navajo himself, he was very helpful in explaining his culture and environment to me. Shopping was done not at a trendy shop called "The Trading Post" but at a real trading post. He was aware of Tareyton's advertising that invited people to look for the white ring that encircled Tareyton's filter. The ring, he explained, was a very important icon to the Navajos symbolizing forever, life, infinity and several other positive concepts.

Using my notes, I wrote several commercials and, after client approval, sent the spots in the form of scripts for the announcer to read. Since there was no written Navajo language, my scripts were sent to the radio host in English. He would translate them directly into Navajo during his broadcast.

I didn't think about them until several weeks later when the account executive on the Taryeton account dropped into my office with some audiocassettes in his hand. They were tapes of my radio commercials...recordings taken directly off the air as they were broadcast. "Would you like to hear your spots, Don?" he asked, smiling. "Darn right," I replied. These were some of my first commercials...I had to hear them.

He popped one into a cassette deck and hit the "Play" button. As the tape started, his smile split into a grin. They were in Navajo. My smile faded. "Very funny." But then he held out three sheets of paper. They were translations of the commercials from the Navajo back into English made by the curator of New York's Museum of the American Indian.

As I read them, I turned pale. The translation from English to

Navajo and back into English again had brought some changes in my copy that would probably put me in jail if the Federal Communications Commission spoke Navajo.

Where I had written, "Look for the Tareyton ring for pleasure and relaxation," the English-to-Navajo-to-English translation came back, "The ring of Tareyton will bring you long life and good health." Even in the pre-consumerist, pre-anti-tobacco '60s, that kind of promise could get you into a whole lot of trouble.

Fortunately, the Navajo tribe was apparently somewhat under-represented on the FCC and no charges were ever brought against me, my agency or my client for these somewhat outrageous health claims. But I did learn a lesson. Some years later, when I was asked to write some commercials for Western Airlines that would be translated into Spanish selling their Mexican destinations, I politely begged off.

I had heard those Mexican prisons were sheer hell and I wasn't going to take a chance on spending any time in them.

∞ 4 ∞

CASTING WITHOUT THE COUCH

A director of feature films once told me, "If I've done my casting properly, seventy-five percent of my job is already done."

Casting is crucial to any film but finding the right person for the right role is even more important in a thirty second commercial than in a two hour feature. With only thirty seconds to get across your story, the actors play an even more important role in establishing mood quickly, telling your story and, most important of all, selling your product.

But as crucial as it is, the casting process hasn't changed very much since the days I entered the business. Equipped with the storyboard along with descriptions of the parts to be filled—gender, age, type, etc., the casting person interviews actors and videos them. When the agency people screen the videos, they can fast forward through anyone they don't like which saves enormous amounts of time. But even if computer searches and videos are used in the early stages of casting, ultimately final casting comes down to sitting in a room and meeting the actors face-to-face.

To me it tended to be a grueling routine. In a typical commercial casting session, the actor entered. The director and agency people sat on the other side of a table. The talent stood there nervously while we looked over his or her photos and resumé. A few pleasantries and we were into their first reading. Then, no matter how bad they may have been, I would give the actor a second reading. It irked some people that I gave so much time even to actors who were obviously wrong for the part. But having had many friends who were actors—including an ex-wife— I knew all the preparation, the expectation and often the desperation that went into so many auditions. So I was softer on the talent than was really necessary.

This "hello...please read...we'll call your agent" routine could go on for hours and after a while the faces, photos and performances blurred together. Despite all our good intentions and copious note-taking, it got harder and harder to distinguish one actor from another. That's when a clever actor could help himself by doing something—anything—to break through our boredom and make himself more memorable.

For me, humor worked best.

We were all on the ropes after two days of casting a series of Western Airlines commercials. Running during the winter in Western's cold cities, they would sell the appeal of their warm-weather destinations like Las Vegas or Hawaii. What could be more appealing to someone freezing in a Minneapolis winter than the sight of a warm sunny Los Angeles beach? But we didn't want these commercials to be boring travelogues. They needed a "hook," something that separated them from other commercials and made them more memorable. We thought we had one.

Each spot opened with a loser kind of guy—a "schlep"— donning his muffler, mittens and earmuffs preparing to go out into a blizzard. As our hero is about to open the door, the announcer asks, "What if you woke up tomorrow, and it wasn't winter?"

The schlep steps through the door and, instead of being greeted by ice and snow, voila!, he's in a dugout canoe racing to a Hawaiian beach...or on a Las Vegas diving board...or on the beach in Acapulco. His reaction was crucial. It was a non-speaking part that called for the look of a humorous loser and good pantomime.

We had gone through every schlep in Hollywood and had just about chosen someone for the part. Then in walked actor Art Metrano. He had made something of a name for himself on the Johnny Carson show. Long before David Letterman had offered his Stupid Pet Tricks to the world, Metrano had played a magician who performed stupid magic tricks, all the while accompanying himself by humming the standard variety act song, "Fine and Dandy." His pantomime was very good and he had the look we wanted. We had a mini-conference in the back of the room. It was a dead heat between him and the other finalist.

As I was about to deliver my "we'll call your agent" line, Metrano ad-libbed a stupid magic trick like the ones he had done on the Carson show. Except this one was X-rated and would never have made it on TV. And it was funny as hell. Suddenly, all the tension of the two days dissolved in helpless laughter. His timing was perfect. He had broken the tie and we gave Metrano the part. Humor had carried the day for him.

* * *

Sometimes sex can help get a part...without a casting couch in sight. We had put out a call for a beautiful girl who looked good in a bikini. No lines to deliver, just good looks required. Not a hard commodity to find in Hollywood. It was a red-blooded Brooklyn boy's dream come true...and I was being paid to do this. When I walked through the waiting room filled with girls, my legs grew weak. I had never seen so much beauty so close. It was the cream of California womanhood.

In the casting room we were the perfect picture of professionalism. A girl would come in wearing her street clothes. We'd chat with her briefly, ask her to walk back and forth for us, and then point out the room where she could change into her bikini. Moments later, in her bikini, she paraded for us briefly. And that was it. After a dozen girls, I was hopelessly in love and hopelessly confused. Any one of them would have been great...and we still had at least fifteen more to look at.

During our lunch break, we decried our kid-in-a-candy-store problem. How would we possibly choose a winner? But right after lunch, one of the girls helped us decide. Like the rest, she was stunning and passed the walking back and forth test easily. Then it happened.

When I pointed out the room where she could change into her bikini, she said the room wasn't necessary...and proceeded to change right in front of us. It was a truly memorable moment in advertising. She looked great in the bikini...and out of it. The instant she left the room, we unanimously decided that it was one of the finest auditions we had ever seen.

She got the part.

* * *

There's a dark side to casting. Having been married to an actress who, like so many actors and actresses, had often faced rejection in auditions, I knew how damaging those rejections could be. Some actors can't handle the stress very well and one time I was almost the one who paid the price for it.

One man at a casting session was a successful actor well-known for his role as a desk sergeant in a successful TV show. Every show opened with him briefing the officers about to go on duty, his briefing ending with a signature basso warning to his charges. His talent was recognized not only by the public but also by his peers who voted him an Emmy as Best Supporting Actor one year. That's why I was so surprised when he showed up at a casting call for a TV commercial. But what surprised me even more was his behavior.

Most actors generally do their best acting by appearing to enjoy a casting session. But this man didn't even pretend to like what he was doing...or us. His dark, threatening demeanor made us nervous.

The director and I chatted with him briefly and then asked him to read his part. He wasn't bad at all. I complimented him and gave him a small bit of direction to help his second reading. He started again, then suddenly froze.

"I don't have to put up with this shit," he roared at me and threw the script on the floor.

He stood up, his brawny six-foot-plus frame looming over us. He looked as if he was ready to leap over the table at me. He could have torn me to pieces. There was a pause as if he was deciding what to do then he suddenly spun on his heel and stormed out of the room, hurling a vicious "Fuck you" over his shoulder at us.

Later in the day, when I got back to the agency, I ran into one of our producers, Dick Dwan, and told him about the incident. "If you ever see this guy on a casting sheet," I advised, "run, don't walk. He's absolutely nuts."

"Too late," he replied. "Funny coincidence. The client knows him from his TV show and loves him and I'm using him Friday in a Dodge commercial."

The day after his shoot, Dick dropped into my office.

"Well, how did it go with your guy? Did he behave himself?" I asked.

"Fine...except for one incident. Which happened to be the most expensive shot in the whole commercial."

"And that was...?"

"He was driving the truck along a highway and we had a camera in a helicopter shooting him. I just needed about seven seconds of him driving and around the fifth second he stuck his left arm out of the truck and gave the finger to the camera."

Helicopter filming is notoriously expensive so I knew at that point the budget was in danger.

"He did it again on the second take and ruined it."

"What did you do?"

Dick smiled. "I did what I knew I had to do—I begged. 'Please no finger this time.' And it worked. His arm stayed in the truck and his finger stayed curled on the wheel."

I told this story to an actress friend who had guested in the show the actor had appeared in and she wasn't at all surprised by it. He definitely had a dark side, she said, and it was rumored on the set that he had a police record. If that was true, I'll bet it was for assaulting a casting director.

* * *

Sometimes you can strike casting gold when you least expect it. It happened to me once when we were doing an ad for Western Airlines that highlighted the special services they offered business travelers.

The ad called for a picture of a senior executive-type man sitting in an airline seat. We had hired a photographer to take the picture and were scheduled to look at pictures of prospective models on Monday for a photo session in the middle of the week.

On Saturday night my wife and I were out to dinner with friends, Stan and Marilyn Baker. During the meal, I looked across the table at Stan. He was in his upper fifties and was bald with a fringe of gray hair. Although not matinee-idol handsome, he was very nice-looking and had a ready, infectious smile. As I studied him, I realized he'd be perfect for the ad, a man businesspeople could relate to and like.

When I asked him if he'd be interested in being in an ad, he thought I was kidding.

"Have another glass of wine, Don," he said.

I responded that I was perfectly sober and I really thought he'd be perfect in the ad. He'd appear in newspapers across the western U.S. and would receive a modest modeling fee.

When he realized that I wasn't kidding, he accepted my offer with a big smile and a friendly hug.

The photo shoot went very well. I was there to help Stan relax but it really wasn't necessary. He was comfortable and very natural in front of the camera and the pictures we got were very good.

Two weeks later, the full-page ad starring Stan appeared in the *L.A. Times* and, according to his wife Marilyn, he was thrilled. He went back to the ad time and again, puffed with pride. I found just how proud he was when he and Marilyn invited us over for dinner several weeks later. When I went into the bathroom I saw his ad. He had hung it with pride over the toilet. Although he might have chosen a more dignified showcase, Stan was sure no guest could miss his ad in its coveted location.

But the best was yet to come. The ad and its message were so attractive that at the agency we decided to use Stan's picture in another medium. And so it was that one evening, my wife and I and Stan and Marilyn went to dinner at a restaurant near Los Angeles International Airport. We had come in my car and, after dinner, I apologetically said that I hope they didn't mind but I had to go to the Western Airlines offices to pick up an important package from my client. They were fine with it and several minutes later we were driving down Century Boulevard, the main approach to the airport.

As we neared the airport I said that I needed gas and asked if they minded if I filled up at the station we were approaching. It was fine, Stan assured me. I drove into the station but instead of pulling up to a pump, I stopped in a parking area below a big outdoor billboard.

I got out and suggested Stan get out and stretch his legs. He was puzzled but did it. As he emerged from the car, he followed my gaze that was directed upwards at the giant billboard. He looked up and froze. There he was, 12 feet high on a Western Airlines billboard, his friendly smile glowing down on the thousands of travelers who passed the billboard every day.

It was the surprise of Stan's life. And it definitely beat the display of his ad above his toilet that he had been so proud of until this moment.

* * *

Casting children is a crapshoot. No matter how cute, precocious or adorable they may be in a casting session, there's no telling what they may do in front of a camera...freeze up, giggle, or as happened on one of my kid shoots, make a poo-poo on-camera. That's why we handled a shoot for Congespirin children's aspirin the way we did.

Working on the premise that there's nothing funny about a sick child, we created a simple, direct commercial that showed a series of kids with colds. The voiceover announcer commiserated with moms about how helpless they feel when their children are suffering with a cold. The solution: give them Congespirin to relieve their symptoms. Cut to a beauty shot of the product as hero.

It was a no-nonsense spot and not really very interesting to anyone but a mother with a sick child. Not an award-winner but hopefully it would sell the product to the market we were targeting.

The client liked it and we went into production immediately. They were forecasting what medicine-makers call "a good colds season," meaning a whole lot of people are going to get sick. Bristol-Myers wanted to make sure moms everywhere would run for the Congespirin when their kid's nose started running.

We put out a casting call for kids between the ages of five and ten. These aren't the most fun casting sessions. Stage mothers are drawn like carnivorous flies to the world of commercials and dealing with them at these calls is a lot more stressful than working with their children. As I walked through the waiting room filled with some two dozen children, I looked straight ahead to avoid eye contact with their mothers, some trying to score an extra point or two with a smile that was either coy or seductive.

The session was simple. There were no lines for them to read so we were looking for them to be cute, an easy commodity to find, and to be easy to direct, not so easy. They came in with their mothers, we chatted with each for a moment to get a sense of personality, then asked them to make believe they had a cold. That was it...for six hours. Booooooring!

Because of abuses in the past, rules for shooting children are understandably strict. Without them, under the pressures of production even considerate directors would, at times, push the children too far. But today they can't. Any production in which a child appears must have a social worker present and, depending on the children's ages, a nurse and a tutor. The length of time the children can be on the set is carefully defined and even the duration of a single shot, or "take," is regulated. It's not strange to have a social worker, stopwatch in hand, actually call "Cut!" when the director lets a take run longer than permitted. It was annoying to us at times, but because of the heat of production, I knew it was necessary.

Because of the ages of our actors, we could have each of them on the set for a maximum of fifteen minutes. And because we had no idea what kind of performance each would give once they got on-camera, we decided on a special casting strategy.

There are two kinds of actors, each governed by the rules of a different trade union. Principal performers, as defined by the Screen Actors Guild, are players who are recognizable on-camera and take instructions from the director. Extras, members of the Screen Extras Guild, are background people who are told what to do by someone other than the director, generally an assistant director. From a practical standpoint, principals are paid more for the filming session and receive additional payments when the commercials are aired which extras don't.

We would cast fifteen of the children with the best potential as extras to sit around in the background of the shots playing quietly. We would then move each, one at a time, up to camera center and shoot him or her while they made believe they had a cold. Later, during editing, we could choose the three or four who performed best and use them in the foreground, upgrading them to principals.

The shoot went as expected, the sound stage loaded with kids, moms, social workers, et. al. We followed our plan and it worked well…so well, in fact, that we had an embarrassment of riches—so many cute nose wipings, sniffings and snufflings that we had to make difficult choices. But in the long editing sessions, we chose the four best little performers to feature and transformed them from extras to better-paid principals.

The commercial aired and, as predicted, it was a good colds season. Even though we never thought of it as an award-winning commercial, it was a major success. It sold Congespirin so well that Bristol-Myers ended up running it for three consecutive winter cold seasons. Because of that, they weren't the only winner.

Actors are paid additional money—residuals—based on a number of factors including how many markets the commercial runs in and how long it runs. I found out just what that can mean three years later while shooting a commercial for another client.

One of the kids in the commercial we were filming that day, a cute African-American boy, had been in my Congespirin spot. I saw his father and introduced myself as the person who had created that spot. I said that I hoped he did well with the residuals. With a big grin on his face, he grabbed my hand and shook it heartily. He wanted to thank me. They had been receiving residual checks ever since the spot started running three years earlier and the previous month they had received yet another one. That check would serve as the final payment for their son's college education.

I don't think any advertising award I've ever received gave me as much of a thrill as I felt at that moment.

* * *

You'd think that finding a cowboy in Hollywood would be easy. But we were being particular. The commercial we were casting was going to launch Edge shaving gel for S.C. Johnson and we were looking for someone special. We went through nearly twenty hopefuls, many of whom brought their own cowboy hats. There were even a few former stars whose light had dimmed and apparently needed the work.

After hours of professional but predictable cowboys we were getting tired and more than a little grumpy. Then in walked Bob Ridgely. Having shot my spots mostly in New York, I had never seen him before but apparently he was well known around Hollywood. He wore a cowboy hat, and when he recognized our producer from a previous job, he doffed his hat to him. But he was strangely silent. Then, when the producer introduced him to me he spoke.

"Howdie, youngster," he said to me in an impeccable imitation of John Wayne. We all laughed for a moment then I gave him his cue and he delivered his first line in the script.

"Who took mah Edge?" he asked in his very respectable John Wayne imitation. We all laughed at the gag. But it wasn't a gag. He did the whole commercial as the Duke. Thirty seconds later as he read the last line we all cracked up.

"Great audition" the director said. "Now try it straight, Bob."

"Wait a second," I said. "Why can't he do it as John Wayne?"

"Because Wayne would sue our asses, that's why," said our account executive.

"Maybe not," I said. "Let me find out." Ridgley's reading had given a whole new dimension to the commercial. What a great way to launch Edge...if we could do it legally without getting our asses sued.

I called our agency attorney in New York and described the situation. Could Wayne go after us if we did this?

The attorney's answer came swiftly. "Not if it was clear that it wasn't really John Wayne on the screen but an actor imitating him."

There were several legal precedents for this, he said. A company had done a series of radio commercials where actors did imitations of famous people like Katherine Hepburn. But because it was radio, the listener could easily believe it was actually

Katherine Hepburn doing the commercial. Hepburn sued and the financial award she received was substantial. But in our case, since the actor was onscreen, it was obvious it wasn't John Wayne. So we were on solid legal ground.

A few days later we shot the commercial with Bob in full John Wayne regalia and attitude. It was one of the funniest and most enjoyable shoots I had ever been on. And what made it even more enjoyable was that we knew we had a winner of a commercial. But there was still one big hurdle ahead: the client had to approve it.

Even though they had approved the storyboard for production, seeing the finished spot could be different. In decades of successfully selling their household products, S.C. Johnson had never done an offbeat commercial like this before. Would they see this, change their minds and put us in hot water?

At Johnson headquarters in Wisconsin, we played it for a senior vice president. When the lights came up, we all turned to him— he had an enormous grin on his face. "Sam has to see this," he said. Sam was Sam Johnson, CEO of the company and heir to the Johnson family fortune.

A few minutes later Sam came into the conference room with a scowl on his face from, as we learned later, a painful phone call he had just endured. Not a good frame of mind to view a humorous, offbeat commercial.

But thirty seconds later, he was smiling. "I love it. Show it again."

After seeing it a second time he insisted that everyone at Johnson see it. And that was the beginning of a whole day of screening the spot for the entire Johnson staff. It was a hit and we were heroes.

More importantly, when the commercial aired on television, it was a hit with consumers and Edge took off, outselling the longtime shaving product leader, Gillette Foamy.

There was a memorable postscript to the story. Not long after the commercial began airing, a friend of Ridgely's called him. His friend was a buddy of John Wayne and the night before he had been at Duke's house watching TV when the commercial came on. Duke laughed. He loved it.

When Bob's friend told him that he knew the actor, Duke drawled this message to relay to Bob: "Tell your friend he has mah voice down pretty good but he oughta work more on mah walk."

∞ 5 ∞

CALIFORNIA HERE WE CAME

Aaah, Los Angeles. In the sixties and early seventies when I was still working in New York, I often would sit in my office and daydream about the palm trees, the sun, the warmth and the women of Southern California. I loved it, especially when the view from my New York office window looked out on the traffic, the crowded sidewalks and the frenetic hubbub that was Manhattan. How could I get out of The Big Apple to LaLa Land?

In those days, it wasn't so difficult—just write a good TV spot and throw in a few palm trees and you had your trip to what we fondly called "The Coast." That was before today's film-the-actors-in-front-of-a-green-screen-and-use-computers-to-put-in-the-palm-trees technology. In those days, if you wanted palm trees and beaches you had to fly to the palm trees and beaches. My clients either never caught on or never cared to, especially if they were going to come along with us on the shoot.

Amazing as it may seem today, in those days for many clients and agencies, budgets seemed to be almost bottomless. I once presented a storyboard for a ninety second commercial to our Xerox clients and they approved it for production on the spot...without even asking how much it would cost. Within a few weeks, a merry band of agency folk was sitting in American Airlines' First Class section winging our way west, champagne flutes raised on high.

Being kissed by the Creative Muse really paid off. On those

California shoots, we worked and played in more-or-less equal measure and many of the stories that came out of those trips were the stuff of legends.

* * *

On a bleak winter day in New York, I had just trudged, frozen, through blocks of dirty slush and yellow snow to my office. I sat there warming up and drying out, daydreaming out loud with art director and friend Peter Tiisler about sun and sand. Several months earlier we had created a commercial for Edge Shave Cream that had successfully launched the product. Now our task was to create a follow-up. When we reluctantly got to work, we started throwing situations back and forth until something struck our creative fancies.

Edge was the first shaving product to come out of the can in the form of a gel rather than as a foam. Because of the superior moisturizing abilities of the gel, it gave a smoother shave with fewer nicks and cuts. (It really is a fine product and I still use it decades after I stopped getting it for free.)

As Peter and I started throwing around situations relating to nicks and cuts, we got off on a wild tangent -- from blood to bats to vampires to Count Dracula. They were nutty ideas but, as happens so often in creative sessions, if you free yourself of the usual inhibitions and go off into the ridiculous, you can often kick off good fresh ideas.

While we were laughing over the silly Dracula bit, we suddenly stopped. Sharks! They love blood. How about the captain of a ship who, worried about blood drawing sharks, orders his scuba divers to shave with Edge. It seemed like a fun premise, far different from the usual, hard-sell mucho-macho commercials for shaving creams that filled the airwaves.

While I went back to my office to hone the forty or fifty words we could use in the 30-second spot, Peter drew the storyboard, the comic strip-like series of pictures that showed how the commercial flowed from start to finish. When we met again later on, Peter showed me the board. The opening frame showed a long shot of a ship in the distance on the ocean with a background of pure blue sky. I thought for a moment, picked up a Magic Marker and put a broad swatch of brown behind the ship.

"What's that?" Peter asked.

"The cliffs of Palos Verdes near Los Angeles," I replied. He laughed. California, here we come!

The client liked the storyboard and three weeks later we were sitting in the California sun—and that was in the days when the sun was still good for you—shooting the spot. My splash of brown Magic Marker had gotten some tired, pale agency people out of cold, dreary New York to the California seashore.

There was an ironic finale to this shoot. I had added the Magic Marker Palos Verde cliffs at the beginning of the storyboard to get us to California. In California, during our preproduction planning with the director, we decided the commercial didn't really need to show a ship at sea to establish it as a working dive ship. The time it would take, the extra boat that would have to be rented to carry the camera and crew as well as the vagaries of shooting on the water would all make it a very expensive opening shot. All this effort and money for a shot that would only be on-screen for three or four seconds.

Instead of all that, a shot of the deck of a ship with the right props showing—dive tanks, coiled ropes, etc.—would instantly say dive boat. And it would do it a lot less expensively. So we decided to shoot the whole commercial on a boat tied up in San Pedro harbor, just south of Los Angeles. The other boats and boating activity in the harbor would add good background color to the piece.

But on the day of our shoot, when we got on location we found the harbor was so commercial and sleazy-looking we didn't want it to be seen. So to avoid showing any of it, we shot everything with close-ups and low angles of the actors with nothing but the sky in the background. By the time we got to the final edit, it turned out that we really didn't have to shoot it in California. We probably could have shot most of it in my Manhattan apartment and no one would have known the difference.

But we never could have done that...we would have missed out on a great trip to California.

* * *

It was on one of our California commercial filming trips that Peter Tiisler and I decided to really go California.

What says California more than surfing? Never mind that neither one of us had ever touched a surfboard let alone ridden one. But we both were skiers and couldn't imagine that surfing could be much harder than schussing down a New England ski trail strapped onto a pair of skittish skis.

We were free the day before the commercial shoot and so, leaving the luxury of our Beverly Hills Hotel suites and armed with totally undeserved confidence, we drove south from Los Angeles. We paralleled the coastline until we saw a lovely beach that looked to our New York eyes to have a nice surf breaking onto the shore. We parked by a beachside surf shop and walked in.

"We'd like to rent a pair of surfboards," Peter said.

"You guys have experience?" the shop owner asked.

"Not a lot," Peter responded. Technically that was accurate since Peter rightly assumed that "not a lot" was just a comfortable way of saying "none."

The owner sized us up and gave us each a board. As we tucked our boards under our arms and started to leave the shop, the owner inquired, "Don't you want to use some surf wax?"

"Oh sure," I said. "I guess we're so anxious to get out into the surf again that we forgot."

He handed each of us a cake of wax and we turned over our boards and thoroughly waxed the bottom of each.

"Have fun out there," he called after us, a big grin on his face. As we found later, we should have paid more attention to that grin.

Standing on the edge of the water, Peter and I watched the other surfers, checking out their techniques for paddling out on their bellies, turning around towards shore, catching a wave, then standing up and obviously enjoying the swift ride to shore. They made it look so easy.

It wasn't. Peter went first, struggling to paddle out against the incoming waves.

When he was beyond the breaking wave, he managed to turn his board around and then, as the waves started to carry him shoreward, tried to stand up. He barely made it to one knee then slipped face-first onto his board and off into the water. I laughed like crazy but then it was my turn. I didn't do much better although I did avoid the hard face plant onto the board that he had suffered.

For a second try we both paddled out and turned around in time to catch an incoming wave. We both fell into the water and our boards beat us to the beach. On the next attempt we both hit the water and our boards hit us. After several more tragic tries, as we dragged ourselves and our boards out of the water we faced the surf shop owner and several of his friends. They had been watching us with barely contained laughter.

Grinning, he asked, "You guys really don't have a lot of experience, do you?"

"Not a lot," I responded.

"We don't have any," Peter admitted. "I guess you could tell from watching us out there in the water."

"I didn't have to wait till I saw you in the water to tell. I knew it before you left the shop."

"How could you tell?"

"I knew you didn't know shit about surfing the second you

guys started to apply the wax to the bottom of your boards. Skiers put wax on the bottom of your skis to make them more slippery. Surfers put our wax on the top of the boards to make them less slippery so that our feet can get a better grip."

"Why didn't you tell us that you knew we were phonies?"

"Because," he said, "we thought it might be fun to watch you guys floundering around."

"I bet it was fun," Peter said dourly.

"Not fun. Hysterical. You guys were great!"

At that, the surfer group he had gathered to watch us let out a big cheer. Peter and I were a hit...not as surfers. As New York jerks.

* * *

One of the joys of shooting commercials in California was where we stayed—the fabled Beverly Hills hotel. Standing pink and proud on Sunset Boulevard, its rooms and restaurants had housed and fed Hollywood's greatest dating back to the days of Douglas Fairbanks, Mary Pickford and Charlie Chaplin. When you stood there waiting for the valet to deliver your car, you could easily be standing next to Marilyn Monroe or Gregory Peck waiting for theirs. You could walk into the Polo Lounge and find Milton Berle and Danny Thomas trading wit and wisecracks. The hotel made even the most difficult commercial shoot easier so we all looked forward to our stays there.

And so it was that one evening Peter Tiisler and agency producer Peter Grounds arrived at the reception desk of the hotel after a long flight from New York. They had reserved mid-priced rooms but the clerk informed them that they had no rooms available at that price. Instead, the hotel would be putting them into one of their bungalows at the room rate they had requested until the kind of rooms they wanted were available.

Peter Grounds was elated. He knew that the bungalows at the Beverly Hills were their ultra-deluxe accommodations complete with fireplaces and open bar and cost what would today be the equivalent of $2,000 a night. Tiisler, on the other hand, was furious. To him, a bungalow was a shanty like he and his parents had stayed in on their summer trips to the Catskill Mountains and featured creaking floors, patched window screens and a curly roll of sticky dead-fly-covered flypaper hanging from an exposed rafter. He leaned his husky 6'5" frame over the counter and was about to threaten the clerk angrily when Grounds saved the day— and the bungalow—with a hard step on his friend's toes.

"We'll take it," he smiled to the clerk and they were instantly bungalow-bound. When the bellhop opened the door to their newfound palace, it was every bit as grand as advertised— fireplace, bar, luxurious beds and all.

They celebrated their good fortune with a nice meal in the hotel's Polo Lounge along with an expense-account-sized series of drinks. It was near midnight when they left the Lounge and headed to the bungalow area. When they got there, they had a problem— they were so drunk that all the bungalows looked alike.

After sizing up all the possibilities, Grounds staggered up to the entrance of one of them and proclaimed confidently that he was positive that this one was theirs.

He took out his key and as he was fumbling with the lock, the door flew open. A huge bathrobed figure was silhouetted in the doorway. In a booming and very annoyed voice the man enquired, "Can I help you?"

As he backed off sheepishly, Grounds realized that, of all the guests to intrude on and irritate, he had picked Orson Welles.

* * *

Peter Grounds was the star of another memorable Beverly Hills Hotel moment. In those days, the Polo Lounge was the place to see and be seen...and heard. In the pre-cell phone days, instead of having a telephone in every booth, each booth had its own telephone plug. If a call came in for a person the staff knew, they would bring a phone to their booth and connect it for them.

But if the call was for someone they didn't know, one of the hosts would walk through the Lounge with a phone calling out their name. When the call recipient waved his or her hand, the host brought the phone to their booth, plugged it in and handed it to them.

And so it was that one night several of us, including Peter Grounds, were having dinner in the Lounge. Suddenly, the steady hubbub hum of the room was broken by the repeated cry, "Phone call for Grounds. Phone call for Mr. Peter Grounds." As the host carrying the phone passed our table, Peter tried to get his attention. But the host continued through the Lounge waving the phone and calling out Peter's name. As he passed our booth a second time, Peter waved at him more vigorously. The man stopped next to Peter but instead of handing him the phone, leaned down and whispered to him.

"There's no phone call for you, Mr. Grounds. I'm just trying to make you a little more famous around here." And with that and a quick wink he continued for one more name-calling circuit before putting down the phone and going silent. It turned out that he knew Peter from previous trips and tips and wanted to have some fun.

I capped it by loudly asking Peter for his autograph. Eyes turned to the smiling—and blushing—Mr. Grounds. Another semi-star-studded evening at the Beverly Hills Hotel.

Peter's phoney phone call was just one of several instances when The Beverly Hills Hotel showed that they seemed to have had a soft spot for Peter.

One evening three of us were waiting for Peter in the lobby. We had reservations at one of Los Angeles' finer restaurant so we didn't want to be late lest they give away our hard-to-get tables. Peter finally showed up five minutes late with a red face and sweat dripping off his forehead.

He had gotten a call on the wall phone in the bathroom that had really upset him. The company producing the commercial we were going to shoot had raised the price because of some unanticipated expenses. Peter told us he was so angry that he had slammed the phone down on the receiver hard…so hard that he had ripped the phone off the wall along with a big chunk of the wall.

There's going to be hell to pay, along with big bill, he said.

But there was nothing he could do about it and we went out to a sumptuous dinner along with sumptuous glasses of wine.

We got back to the hotel about three hours later and retired to our rooms. As I was brushing my teeth, my phone rang. It was Peter. He was laughing hysterically.

"You're not going to believe this, Don. But while we were gone they had repaired the wall and reinstalled the phone."

Not a word was said by the hotel about the phone and when we checked out several days later, there was no charge on Peter's bill. We never figured out why the Beverly Hills Hotel treated him so well so often. But I thought that it would be a good idea to stick close to him while I was at the hotel. Maybe some of his charm might rub off on me.

* * *

The sharks that I occasionally had to deal with on Madison Avenue were nothing compared to the real ones I swam with one day in order to shoot a commercial.

The commercial we had written for Xerox opened on a school of fish swimming past the camera. We had created it hoping to get a trip from New York to the Caribbean or at least to Florida. But the production company we had hired to shoot the spot had experience in underwater work and warned us that the chances of corralling a school of fish in the wild and having them swim obediently in front of the camera on cue was a real long shot...nearing the impossible. The best place to get the shot, they said, was in an aquarium and their best recommendation was at the Marineland of the Pacific south of Los Angeles. Never ones to say "No" to a California trip, we got budget approval from the client and off we flew westward into the sun.

When we arrived at Marineland the day of the shoot, we were delighted to look into their main tank and see it filled with all sorts of colorful fish, large and small. Now all we had to do was to get them to swim before our underwater cameraman. That was going to be easy. The aquarium had professional divers who fed the fish daily. They knew the fish and their behaviors and could do it easily.

But it wasn't to be. There was a union problem. The divers were hired to feed and care for the fish, not herd them in front of movie cameras. Their union rules and insurance coverage wouldn't allow them to help us. So there we were. Water, water everywhere but no one to go into it to get the fish to cooperate.

But wait! There was someone on our team who had scuba experience who might be able to help. Me. I had done scuba diving in YMCA pools in New York and in the Cayman Islands in the Caribbean. But could I coax fish to swim by the camera? I had no idea. The only way to tell was to do it.

The divers, sorry for their inability to dive for us, were happy to loan me the scuba gear I needed—a wet suit, regulator and tank of air.

But another problem reared its not-so-pretty head. The air bubbles trapped in a wet suit that insulate the diver against the cold water also create buoyancy and tend to carry a diver towards the surface. To stay at any desired level, a diver wears a weight belt containing small bars of lead. The amount of lead is adjusted depending on the diver's weight and the depth he wants to stay at.

The divers handed me one of their weight belts. It was heavily weighted to keep them on the bottom of the tank as they walked around feeding the fish. But to herd fish, I couldn't be on the bottom so I started to remove one of the weights. The diver stopped me. "Sorry, pal," he said. "You can't remove any of the weights."

"But…" I started to protest.

"Sorry, the weights have to stay on the belt."

So with full scuba gear and a weight belt with 20 pounds more lead than I needed, I started down the ladder into the Marineland main tank. I pushed off from the ladder and immediately plummeted to the bottom.

The bottom was sandy and when my finned feet touched it they kicked up a blinding sand cloud. In a few moments the sand began to settle and, as the water cleared, I found myself staring into the

Me at a California aquarium getting ready to herd fish toward the camera for a commercial…a duty not in my job description.

open, tooth-filled mouth of a moray eel. He seemed (to me, at least,) upset that his cozy stone cavern was being disturbed by this large, strange-looking advertising guy.

Eager to get out of there, I pushed off from the bottom and made a very non-earthshaking realization—with the weight I was carrying, to stay off the bottom and coax the fish before the cameras I would have to swim constantly using my hands and flipper-covered feet.

The diver had assured me that the sharks were mild-mannered sand sharks and I had nothing to fear from them. But those teeth still looked awfully sharp and I found it hard to trust my precious lifeblood to the assurances of a stranger. However, I had no choice and just trusted to faith that he was right.

And so we began the shoot. At the hand signal from the cameraman (who was wearing the properly weighted belt he had brought with him from New York), I did my best to herd a group of fish toward the camera.

But the fish wouldn't cooperate. They dispersed before he got the shot he wanted and I got a visual thumbs-down from him.

Take two. Constantly using my flippers to stay off the bottom, I waved my arms frantically to corral the fish and move them past the camera. Another thumbs down and it was back to the start.

It took over a dozen takes and encounters with more moray eels, poisonous lionfish and sharks before the cameraman gave me the dream signal: thumbs up. We had gotten the shot. Finally.

I swam to the side and, with my last drop of energy, hauled myself up the ladder and collapsed on the deck of the tank. The cheers and applause of my team and the production crew felt good. But I didn't. I was exhausted and lay on the deck for over five minutes before finally standing up and doffing the scuba gear including the dreaded overweight weight belt.

We had gotten the shot we needed for the opening of the commercial. All five seconds of it.

* * *

One of the reasons filming in California was so attractive was getting there. My agency, Needham Harper & Steers, had a liberal travel policy that is probably not very common today: people at the vice president level were entitled to fly First Class, a luxury I enjoyed enormously. Fine champagne and gourmet food served by attractive flight attendants—then known by the more sexist term "stewardesses"—was a perk I reveled in along with my advertising compadres who flew with me. It was on one of these flights that an associate could have added a credit to his resume that he didn't deserve.

On a flight to Los Angeles, I was traveling with a talented editor, Pat de Rosa, who would edit the commercial we were going to shoot. The inflight movie they were showing was *My Fair Lady*.

In the days before video was used inflight, movies were shown on reels of 16-millimeter film. Halfway through the film, the screen went white. The film had torn. Pat pushed the button that called the flight attendant.

"I can fix it. Editing film is my business," he assured her.

She led him to the compartment where the broken film sat. In a few minutes, with skilled fingers and some Scotch tape, he lined up the perforations in the film, taped the two ends together and threaded the film in the projector. A push of the Start button and the melodic strains of "*On the Street Where You Live*" filled the plane.

As Pat sat down, I leaned over to him and told him he could have a great reward for saving the day. "Now you can put in your resume that you edited *My Fair Lady*."

To his credit, he declined.

∞ 6 ∞

THOSE DARN CLIENTS

As an old ad legend tells it, the agency was presenting a new advertising plan to the client, a successful entrepreneur. A key part of the plan they recommended was to have the radio spots the agency would create run on Sunday afternoons. When the client heard this, he objected.

"Absolutely not," he said. "No one will ever hear those commercials."

"Why not?" asked the agency representative.

"Because," the client responded, "everybody knows that on Sunday afternoon everyone's out playing polo."

The Sunday radio schedule was killed.

Whether fact or fable, the story illustrates the golden rule of advertising—and of business: "He who has the gold, rules." In advertising, the client is king and calls the tune, even if he or she is tone deaf. As anybody who's been in business long enough knows, we each get our share of wonderful clients and our share of jerks. The difficult clients bring us our share of frustration but along with that, hopefully they bring us our share of chuckles.

* * *

It's said that everybody has an opinion about advertising. That doesn't matter except if that opinion is from your client. But it gets tougher to accept when the client's spouse also has a vote. That's what I once faced when I was working on the Yellow Pages account.

I didn't create it but I was lucky to be able to contribute to the classic "Let Your Fingers Do the Walking Through the Yellow Pages" campaign. My creative partner and I were given the job of writing a Yellow Pages television spot. We were responsible for creating the first two thirds of the commercial because the ending of every spot was standard. To demonstrate just how easy using the Yellow Pages made shopping, with the well-known Yellow Pages jingle playing in the background we would show an open Yellow Pages directory as a woman's fingers walked across the page and ended up pointing to one of the ads.

The filming went very smoothly. The hand model we used was very professional, her hands were beautiful and her fingers walked across the page perfectly. We filmed the ending in only two takes.

We showed the finished commercial to our client who approved it and a week later it had its first airing on national television. The next morning, our account executive in charge of the Yellow Pages account got an angry phone call from the client. Apparently, the client's wife had seen the commercial and was disgusted.

"This commercial is filthy," she exclaimed to her husband. Her reasoning: if the woman's fingers were supposed to be legs then the hand/woman was naked. The hand should at least be wearing a skirt.

Everyone in our group laughed and thought it was nuts. But not our account executive. He was the one who had to face the client with the dirty-minded wife. In advertising, a good rule of thumb is "don't ever tell a client who is spending $15 million a year that his wife is nuts."

So we reshot the ending to everybody's satisfaction. Instead of the woman's fingers walking across the page all the way to the ad, we had her fingers take two steps and then slide on her index finger up to the ad. For some unfathomable reason, that appeared to satisfy the client's wife. To her, the commercial was no longer pornographic.

* * *

One of my toughest clients was an automotive account. While I worked on it, I was really under the gun—possibly, I thought, even a .38 special.

In the auto industry, there are three classes of advertisers: the manufacturer (commonly called "the factory"), the dealer and the local dealer association. The association serves an important purpose for the dealers. By pooling their advertising dollars and, helped by money the factory allocates for dealer advertising, the dealers can make a bigger impact in the community they serve.

But for an ad agency, working with dealer associations can be tough. First, the dealers often seem to be fighting the manufacturer and since there was a representative of the factory at every dealer meeting, there were a lot of chips on a lot of shoulders. The result was that the meetings were often very contentious. So I was a little conflicted when I got the assignment to work with the New York/New Jersey dealer association of a leading American auto manufacturer.

I saw the dynamics of the association at the first meeting I attended. It seemed more like a Mafia meeting than a gathering of successful businessman. I wouldn't have been surprised if they had kissed each other's cheeks in greeting when they came in. During the meeting in which they discussed an upcoming promotion for the New York metropolitan region, every one of them had an opinion. It would have been a free-for-all if it wasn't for the president of the dealer association. He was quiet but strong and all the members deferred to him. There was a distinct fragrance of Mafia about him and I could tell at that first meeting that if you crossed him, whether you were a dealer or an ad agency guy, you could be in serious trouble.

Our assignment: the manufacturer would be sending the dealers in the area a unique shipment of cars. They would be specially equipped and priced and would all have similar paint schemes...ugly ones: yellow and black. Our job was to create an advertising campaign that would drive traffic to their showrooms.

We had three weeks to prepare a campaign that would either knock the dealers out or knock me off the account. After a week of going up blind alleys, we hit on something. What's yellow and black and runs all over? Bees. That was our theme and we created newspaper ads, radio commercials and a television spot for them. To cut through the advertising babble we came up with a unique buzzing-bee sound that would appear in all the radio and TV spots.

Then came the tough part—I would have to present this advertising campaign to the dealers at the next meeting. The day of the meeting, when I stood up to begin my pitch all I saw was twelve pairs of Mafioso-esque eyes around the table. And at the opposite end of the conference table, the wolf-like eyes of the association president seemed to burn holes in my shirtfront. I had the feeling that if it didn't go well, that night, instead of wearing my woolen bedroom slippers I would be wearing a pair of cement overshoes.

I started out playing the buzzing bee sound, the aural signature of the campaign. Then, one by one, I showed the newspaper ads and the storyboard for the television commercial and then played the radio commercial we had recorded in the agency. During the entire 20 minutes I got no feedback from the group... no frowns, no smiles. Nothing.

As I sat down, the silence continued. Not one of the dealers volunteered his reaction. Instead, every one of them turned to the president. Expressionless, he looked up and down at the men at the table and then finally, in his impeccable New York accent he spoke one of the most wonderful sentences I ever heard.

"I don't know about you guys, but I think this is the best

fuckin' car advertisin' I ever seen."

I breathed for the first time in 10 minutes. Our work had gotten the green light so the dealers chimed in with their approval.

We went on to produce the advertising I had presented and the campaign was wildly successful, exceeding sales projections by over 25%.

But the high point of the whole adventure was that meeting when I presented the campaign. Because even if I wasn't carried out of the room on the dealers' shoulders, I knew that at least I wouldn't be dumped into the Hudson River that night.

* * *

One of the liveliest perennial debates in advertising concerns the shelf life of an ad campaign. How long do you run it before it gets tired? On the one side there's the advantage of repetition—the more a reader is exposed to an ad campaign, the better the chances of its getting its message across.

On the other side of the equation is the concern that, at a certain point, familiarity will begin to breed contempt and the reader will commit advertising's most dreaded act: turning the page or clicking the left mouse button. Lots of research has been done but no meaningful formula has ever been devised to tell just when wear-out is reached and it's still a seat-of-the-pants judgment call.

There's one group that can suffer from ad fatigue faster than any other: the clients. Tom Dillon, then chairman of BBDO, told me about a visit he had with the president of Campbell's Soups, one of the agency's most important clients. He was sitting in the client's office discussing their advertising program when the president complimented the agency on a really fine series of ads for Campbell's red-and-white label soup line. But, he said, looking at the beautifully laminated ads on his wall, didn't Tom think they were getting a little tired and new ones should be created?

Tom looked at the ads and sighed. They may have been hanging in the president's office for weeks, but not a single one of them had yet run in a magazine.

Yes, they had been overexposed. But only in the president's office.

* * *

At BBDO/West in Los Angeles we learned that a large California-based account was looking for an advertising agency. Even better, it was a Japanese company, something we sorely missed in our Los Angeles office. Hitachi was looking for an ad agency to handle advertising for its television set division. We let them know that we were both capable and interested and met with them for an input session to learn more about them and the products they would like help in marketing.

At the meeting, they explained how their television sets had a strong advantage over the competition's. Using new advances in electronics, they were able to design a set that ran much cooler than other television sets. Because heat is a great enemy of electronics, Hitachi assured us, their sets would operate better and last longer.

When pitching a new account there are two kinds of presentations. One is called a capabilities presentation. In that, you sell your experience and what you've done for other clients giving case histories and showing the good creative work you did for them.

The second kind of presentation is a lot more expensive and a lot more work. In this version, you actually produce creative work on the prospect's behalf, generally done speculatively with no remuneration. We really wanted the Hitachi account and so decided that we would gamble the time and money and do spec creative work for their presentation.

The product advantage we would be selling for Hitachi's cool-running design they called Polacolor...pola as in polar bear. The challenge we faced was how to express it in a way that was interesting and would stop viewers long enough to hear the story.

As with most creative challenges, we spent a lot of time throwing out ideas that merited throwing out. We knew there was a good way of telling their story lying in wait for us somewhere. We just had to find it.

Then came that too-rare but wonderful "Ah-hah!" moment.

I blurted out an idea. "A guy is standing between the television set and a barbecue. He looks at the camera and explains to the viewing audience.

"This is a hibachi." (He points.) "This is a Hitachi." (He points.) "The hibachi is hot (touches it and quickly withdraws his hand) but the Hitachi is not." Then, smiling, he puts his hand paternally on the television set.

The idea was humorous and easy-to-understand. Everybody in the agency liked it instantly, so much so that we decided that, rather than just showing them a storyboard drawing of the commercial, we would spend the money to actually shoot it.

We rented a stage in a studio, hired an actor and spent a day shooting and editing the commercial. We loved it. But we didn't count. Hitachi would have to fall in love with it.

We were invited to Hitachi's offices to make our presentation and when we arrived we were surprised and pleased to find that the Japanese president of Hitachi North America would be attending.

Everything in our presentation was designed to lead up to the grand finale, the unveiling of our new Hitachi commercial. One by one, our executives got up and proudly proclaimed our capabilities, how well-equipped and well-experienced we were to help Hitachi hit a grand slam with their new line of television sets.

Then it was my turn to present the creative work. I stood up and, trying to maintain an air of understatement, quietly introduced what we hoped would be Hitachi's new groundbreaking TV commercial.

The lights went out and the videotape rolled. As the announcer began "This is a hibachi...this is a Hitachi," we all smiled proudly.

It was all over in 30 seconds. We looked over the sea of mostly Japanese faces to see the rewarding smiles. But there were none. Then I looked over to the person who counted most, the Hitachi president. He was sound asleep.

The marketing director stood up, smiled and thanked us very much. They would be making their decision shortly and would let us know. Our hour-long drive back to the office felt like five. What had we done wrong?

Within a week we found out. We were told that, in our cleverness, we had made a major cultural boo-boo. Apparently, to the Japanese the hibachi is associated with the lower classes and Hitachi would never want to be associated with it. The commercial was Dead On Arrival.

As for the president's snooze? It wasn't boredom. It was fatigue. An hour before our meeting started, he had stepped off a 15-hour flight from Singapore and was exhausted. However, we reasoned later on, it was just as well that he had dozed. If he had stayed awake we'd just have had another vote against our culture-defying commercial.

* * *

It's not often that a few words can change your life. Seven of them changed mine dramatically. And I wasn't the one who said them.

Xerox was the most sought-after advertising account of the year, if not the decade. It wasn't because of its budget, which was modest, but because of the high caliber of the creativity in its advertising. It was considered a showcase account, one that's highly visible and gives its agency a chance to show off its best creative work to the world.

The previous ad agency for Xerox had developed marvelously inventive, refreshing ads and commercials and, equally important, Xerox had bought their ideas. The advertising had won awards, pleased the Xerox sales force (vital to any successful ad campaign), and had elevated this unknown company with an unknown product into a Fortune 500 corporation.

But, while the creativity continued to percolate, agency and client personalities clashed. And so one day Xerox announced that it was looking for a new agency and the entire ad community started to breathe heavily.

At Needham Harper & Steers/NY, we had been pursuing new business constantly but for a year the scoreboard registered nothing but goose eggs. Our recent attempts to win new accounts had been annoyingly and consistently unsuccessful. We had ended up as a bridesmaid at some half-dozen new business pitches in the previous twelve months. To think we stood a chance of getting the single most prestigious—and most sought-after—account in the industry was a stretch, to say the least.

But what the hell, our management thought. The first step was just filling out a long Xerox questionnaire like the other forty contenders.

I never knew who in the agency filled it out for us but whoever did sure gave good questionnaire. We were told by Xerox that we had made the first cut. They would like to visit our New York offices.

Xerox wasn't asking for the agencies to do speculative creative work for them to help them decide. Instead, they would make their decision based on who we were and what we had done for other clients.

Needham's management took a gamble for the meetings. The standard, typical agency new business presentation is invariably smooth as a baby's behind: reels of agency TV commercials are shown, marketing successes are recounted in song and story using carefully prepared PowerPoint presentations. These shows can be very strong and effective.

But from their contacts in the industry and talks with Xerox executives, our management had come to an important conclusion: the Xerox management was very people-oriented compared to most large U.S. corporations. So when they visited us, instead of giving them slick Madison Avenue, we would offer them something unique: regular people.

They would wander around the agency and sit in on a series of unscripted just-sit-around-the-table-and-chat meetings with a few members of each department. Nothing fancy. Just people-to-people stuff. I was flattered when I was chosen to be part of the up-close-and-personal sit-and-chat for the creative department.

On the day of their visit, three of the Xerox people came into the office of my boss, Barry Biederman, and sat down across the table from four of us creative folk. We talked about creative work in general, showed them some of the work we'd done and told them the story behind the creation of each one. Fifteen minutes later they were on to their next chat. It was all very casual and low key. No hard selling and there were even a few chuckles. It was very unorthodox for a big-time new business pitch.

And apparently the Xerox folks enjoyed their visit with us. They liked our work and had liked the chemistry. Incredibly, ne'er-do-well Needham had made it to the finals!

The last step was for six of us to fly to their headquarters in Rochester, New York to meet key Xerox executives. It was here that those seven words won us the most coveted account of the decade. And changed my life.

We met several officers of the corporation including the fabled and much-beloved Joe Wilson, the man who actually created the company and, along with it, the entire copier industry. All went businesslike and affable until the end of a short meeting with the Xerox marketing director who had been our chief liaison with Xerox during the process.

He looked at his watch and confided to us that he had a problem. "I have a meeting to go to and your competition is in the building. I just don't know what to do with them while I'm busy."

Without skipping a beat, Graham Rohrer, an older, pipe-puffing member of our team, offered, "Bring them in here."

"What will you do with them?" asked the Xerox man.

"We'll kick the shit out of them," Graham responded.

There was a stunned silence...then uncontrollable laughter. Including from the client. It was an honest feeling no one would ever express…except Graham.

It took over a minute for everybody to recover their composure. After all the nervous formality, the ice had been broken. And that tipped the scales. Like so many important choices in business, agency decisions often come down to the fact that people like to do business with people they like. A few days later it was announced that Needham Harper & Steers had been awarded the Xerox account.

My career was never the same after that. As everyone who worked on the Xerox account found, the client was ready and eager to accept good creative work. That allowed me and my teammates to be creative, strengthen our portfolios of work, win a few awards...and get much-appreciated raises.

According to the press, what won Needham the account was our good track record. But what really won it were Graham's seven words that had won their hearts. And changed my life.

A few years after I left Needham, I learned that Graham had done it again. The agency was pitching a large new account and, if they got it, Graham would be the senior account executive.

The pitch appeared to be going well when the client asked Graham an important question: if they awarded the agency their account, how much of his time would he devote to it?

Graham responded, "100% of my time."

Client: "Then what would you tell your other clients?"

Graham: "The same thing."

Graham's candor proved once and for all that there really is such a thing as truth in advertising.

* * *

It's only natural—an advertiser doesn't like its ad agency handling the advertising of one of its competitors. To do its job well, an agency has to know many of a company's trade secrets, their plans and products for the future and any problems they may have. That knowledge in the hands of a competitor can be valuable so clients understandably insist on having exclusivity in their product or service category.

That presented a problem for a major agency like BBDO—they handled clients in so many product and service categories that finding one that's open to them was difficult. That's why, when Kawasaki Motorcycles announced that it was looking for a new agency, our New York headquarters jumped—we had no motorcycle client so the category was open to us. And because Kawasaki was California-based, our Los Angeles office would make the pitch and, if we won, would get the account.

One problem: not one person in our office owned a motorcycle, rode one regularly or even knew very much about them. But that wasn't going to stop us. On Madison Avenue I had done advertising for a feminine hygiene product and naturally had had very little experience using it. None, actually. If you get an assignment for a product you're not familiar with, you just learn about it. And learning about motorcycles is a hell of a lot more fun than learning about Maxi Pads.

But we didn't just want to read about motorcycles. We wanted to ride them. The experience would help us create better advertising and, if we photographed our riding for the presentation, could give us credibility in the client's eyes.

So we enlisted the help of Petersen Publishing, publishers of *Motorcycle Magazine*. They, of course, were eager to help since, if we got the account, we would buy ad space in their magazine. They had a number of motorcycles they could loan us and, better yet, their Petersen Ranch north of Los Angeles gave us a place to play that was free from traffic and the steely stares of the California Highway Patrol.

On the appointed day, six people from my creative department along with the three account executives who would work on the account gathered at the ranch, equipped with ill-fitting borrowed boots and gloves. The Petersen folks supplied everything else—the bikes, the helmets and, most important of all, the instructions. We were all novices so they had to start from scratch—how to start the bike, how to shift gears, and, most important, how to stop it. (You hit the rear brakes first. Hit the front ones and there's chance you'll go ass-over-teakettle over the handlebars.)

Then it was time. We all fired up our engines, shifted into low gear and started running into trees, rocks and each other. It was at least a half hour before I could take any presentable pictures that would show off our motorcycling skills to Kawasaki.

As they say, a little knowledge can be dangerous. And we had very little knowledge. We were probably saved from serious mishaps because a) the ranch was hilly so we couldn't really wind up the machines to full throttle and b) lots of just plain luck.

I came close to a big one when I faced a hill with a road at the top. I had seen Evel Knievel do a hill climb so of course I knew how. At the bottom, I gunned the engine, slipped the bike into gear and launched up the hill. But I had forgotten one thing that Knievel did in his hill climbs—he stopped at the top. As I came to the crest I still had the throttle fully wound. I had assumed I would jump the little road and would land softly on the other side. But I suddenly realized something I might have thought of earlier—on the other side of the road was the downhill side of the hill I had just climbed. I went airborne over the road and looked down at the steep drop below me. That's where the other factor kicked in—dumb luck.

Fortunately, my bike's rear wheel hit first so I was thrown off to the side rather than dangerously over the handlebars. When I stopped bouncing, I looked up at the road I had just leaped over and there was my team, applauding wildly and smiling snidely.

But by the end of the day we had really learned a lot about motorcycling. And I had gotten a series of pictures to show Kawasaki our fantastic cycling skills. They would be impressed by the pictures...as long as I didn't show the 90% of them that would embarrass us.

As you can see, the preparation for our presentation to the client was a problem. But the meeting itself was even worse. My boss in New York really wanted us to win the account and so he came out to Los Angeles to be in on our presentation.

Bad move. Our track record in new business pitches was pretty good. But having him in our meeting was a disaster. Each of us who would have responsibility for a portion of the Kawasaki account knew what we had to do. But my boss believed that to win the account, he would have to guide us. So throughout the meeting he stood behind us prodding us to speak when he thought it was appropriate and signalling to shut us down when he thought we were talking too much.

It was very awkward for us and when the meeting was over I thanked our prospect as if all was roses...even though, to me it was more poison ivy.

Not long afterwards we were informed, not surprisingly for us, that we didn't get the account. I admired their honesty. They had liked the work we had done for other clients and liked what we said about what we were thinking about their future. But they weren't crazy about that guy who stood behind each of us coaching us and treating us like ventriloquist's dummies.

* * *

Going after new business can be difficult, expensive and, when the client is difficult, often very painful. One of the best examples was a major company headquartered on the West Coast. It had been renowned in the advertising industry as a tough account. The advertising was overseen by one of its founders who had a reputation as being highly opinionated and difficult to deal with. One year, the firm was voted the most difficult advertising account in the country, a dubious distinction at best.

However, the account had two important attractions to an ad agency. First, it was a very large account that could add mightily to an agency's income. And second, it was a highly visible account whose commercials were seen by millions and so was a great way for an agency to showcase its work to the world.

But the price for pursuing the account could be high as one agency found out. The firm was constantly barraged by requests by agencies for a meeting to pitch their business, most of which were turned down. But one major national agency had an in—a friend on the inside who was able to set up a meeting with the founder along with several of his senior subordinates.

The agency worked for weeks spending hundreds of costly man-hours developing marketing strategies and creating ads and storyboards to illustrate the campaign they would recommend. The cost to the agency was in the tens of thousands of dollars but it would be worth it if they got the account.

The agency's team flew from New York to California and the next day drove to the firm's headquarters. They were heavily armed with portfolios filled with their presentation—impressive examples of the work they had done for other major clients along with all the speculative work they had done for this company.

In the conference room, they faced the executives and, at the head of the giant conference table, the stern-faced senior executive. After a few brief introductions, they began their well-rehearsed presentation. They were proud of their work as they unveiled it with just the right amount of drama, ad after ad and commercial after commercial. There was no reaction from anyone at any point.

When they finished, the agency's team leader wrapped up the pitch and sat down. The silence, as they say, was deafening. Then there was sound…bad sound. Casting brief glances at their boss, person after person began criticizing the work—the strategy was wrong, the advertising wasn't creative enough, they had seen that idea before. There wasn't a positive comment in the bunch.

Finally the executive spoke. His minions had read his reaction to the work correctly. He wasn't very flattering and the agency just sat there and took it. When he had finished, the agency leader stood up and asked if the agency could hold a brief meeting in another office.

Once the team was alone, the emotion was unanimous—anger. To hell with the billing. They all agreed that no matter how big the account was they didn't have to put up with this crap.

Returning to the conference room, the agency leader thanked the attendees very much for their time but respectfully declined to solicit their business any further. They gathered up their work and walked out to their station wagon for the trip to the airport. As they loaded the car with their presentation, the inside executive who had set up the meeting for them ran out to stop them.

"Where are you guys going? They really liked your work," he protested. "Come on back in."

The leader spoke. "If this is the way they act when they like the work, I don't want to be anywhere near them when they don't."

And with that they climbed into the car to start their long, painful journey back to New York. They didn't have the account but at least they still had their self-respect.

* * *

In any business, it's always rewarding when a client shows their appreciation for your work. But—and maybe, as a creative person, it's my personal bias—it seems especially rewarding when that appreciation is for creative work that's been done. There's an emotional factor that goes into creative that seems to make any appreciation a client shows for it especially meaningful to me.

A compliment I got from one client was as unusual as it was

unexpected. I was leaving the agency to start my own company and the marketing director for one of my clients, a large regional bank, invited me out to lunch. I was especially flattered because he was, for the most part, a rather unemotional and sometimes brusque person. In the several years I had headed up the creative work on the bank, he criticized freely and made positive comments rarely. For him to take me to lunch was a first.

During our lunch we chatted about the bank, its future and, surprisingly, he showed a genuine interest in my future and that of my new company. That interest was flattering enough but over coffee he gave me a compliment the likes of which I had never heard before.

"You know, Don, you're the first creative person I've ever been able to bring to a meeting at the bank and not have to cover my ears."

As strange as it was, it was the nicest compliment he had ever given me. I'm positive of that because it was the only one.

* * *

The marketing director of the Western Airlines account I served on was the polar opposite. Bert Lynn was a true gentleman. He always acknowledged the work the agency did whether it was a television campaign, a media plan or a marketing presentation we gave to his company.

But there was one compliment he gave me that I was especially proud of because of the deep sincerity with which he gave it. I was at a meeting at the airline's headquarters and had presented some new creative work. I usually stayed for an entire meeting even after I had finished my portion but on that day I had another appointment and had to excuse myself before the meeting was over.

I stood up, made my apology and shook Lynn's hand, preparing to leave. He smiled at me, looked straight into my eyes and said "Don, thank you very much for all your good work."

I was very touched by his sincerity and was quite elated as I drove back to the agency.

A week or so later we had another meeting with him but, because he was recovering from a cold, we held it at his home. As we all sat in his living room discussing a project, his cleaning lady was leaving for the day. As she opened the door she said goodbye to him. He responded immediately.

"'Bye, Maria, and thank you very much for all your good work."

∞ 7 ∞

CREATIVITY: THE MYSTERIOUS MUSE

O ver the years, I've spoken to numerous groups about advertising, creativity and the creative process. And the one question I've been asked at virtually every talk has been, "Where do you get your ideas?"

My answer has always been three simple words: "I don't know."

There are many motivations for coming up with a unique idea—money, awards, promotions, keeping your job, all of the above. But sometimes the single most powerful motivation is the ancient and wonderful Muse: Panic. Facing a short deadline can do one of two things: freeze your brain or inspire you. And, in any situation, you never know which will happen.

An example: one day, Chuck Greenberg, the account executive on the Bristol-Myers account, came rushing into my office. He was in a spot. He had promised the client to deliver a point-of-purchase display piece called a shelf talker for 4-Way Nasal Spray and had totally forgotten to give us the assignment the previous week. A shelf talker is a small card that sits, as its name implies, on a store shelf hopefully calling attention to the product. It has precious little room to show anything but the product and a few brief selling words that will hopefully stop shoppers long enough to at least consider the brand in their purchase decision.

"Give me something. Anything," he pleaded. Recently, he had been having trouble with the client and not delivering this job on time would make things even worse. He was already running late and had to leave in five minutes.

Without even thinking, I blurted out, "Winterize your nose with anti-sneeze."

"What?," he asked.

"That's the line," I replied. I ran into the art director's office and a few minutes later Chuck had a crude drawing of a red nose above a bottle of 4-Way Nasal Spray with my five words. His piece was ready.

He ran out the door to his meeting crying, "I owe you," over his shoulder. Elapsed time from request to layout: six minutes.

He entered my office two hours later, his ever-present cigar glowing as brightly as his smile. The client liked the layout so much that besides using it as a shelf talker, he wanted to run it as a full-page ad in *Reader's Digest* with a 50-cents-off coupon on the facing page. The ad space in the Digest cost around $50,000 in those days -- roughly equivalent to twice that today — of which the agency received a commission of 15 percent.

This successful ad was born out of sheer panic.

The ad ran and pulled such a good response that it was repeated that year and again several times during the following winter colds season. I was told that the agency ultimately received over $30,000 in commissions from the ad...compared to the few hundred dollars they would have gotten as a creative fee for a shelf talker.

All from six minutes of work. If we had had more time, I doubt we would have done any better.

The muse Panic works wonders. Bless her.

* * *

My art director Bill Weinert and I were working on another Bristol-Myers product, Pazo hemorrhoid ointment. The assignment was to write a newspaper ad containing a mail-in coupon good for a free sample of Pazo.

Hemorrhoids are one of those things that are hysterically funny...to anyone who doesn't have them. Creative sessions were fun and the ideas that came out of them were often great but absolutely unusable. A copywriter friend of mine working at another agency on another hemorrhoid treatment, Preparation H, had once come up with a headline, "Kiss your bleeding piles goodbye." That line got a lot of laughs inside the agency but it never saw the light of day.

Neither Bill nor I had hemorrhoids so we were having a grand old time creating headlines that were sometimes funny, usually stupid, always gross.

One we came up with had us on the floor: "Next time your hemorrhoids hurt, you'll kick yourself in the ass for not sending in this coupon."

When Chuck Greenburg, the account executive, came in to check on our progress, we showed him the rough ads we had done to date. He was unmoved. Then, just to lighten things up, we told him our kick-yourself-in-the-ass gag headline. His eyes grinned impishly and he said, "If you lay the ad out, I'll sell it." We saw that he wasn't kidding.

Bill laid out the ad, judiciously editing the headline to read,

"Next time your hemorrhoids hurt, you'll kick yourself for not sending in this coupon." We knew that although the "ass" part was gone, it was definitely implied in spirit. Where else are you going to kick yourself?

Darned if Chuck wasn't right. He sold the ad to Bristol-Myers, they ran it and it pulled the highest coupon redemption in the history of the product.

It taught me a lesson: a big part of creative skill isn't just coming up with ideas. It's recognizing the good ones when you get them.

* * *

After some ten years as a copywriter, I hoped I had built some kind of good record for coming up with ideas for opening commercials. What I didn't know was that I had developed something of a reputation for closing them.

I discovered it one day when my office phone rang. It was my boss, Irv Sonn, the agency creative director asking me to come to his office. As I walked down the hall, of course the first thing I thought of was, "What did I screw up to be called to the boss' office?"

Seated in his office were two friends of mine, an art director-copywriter creative team that also worked on the Xerox account. Irv held up a storyboard of a Xerox commercial they had just shown him.

"These guys have come up with a good commercial for the first 25 seconds but they have no idea how the hell to end it."

The next moment I discovered a reputation I never knew I had.

"Could you write one of your charming endings for it?"

"My what?" I asked.

"Your charming endings," Irv explained. "Your spots always have some kind of good zapper at the end. This spot needs one."

I had no idea that I was known for creating good endings but I was nonetheless flattered. But I was also a little chagrinned. Being asked to fix a fellow creative team's work put me in a very embarrassing position. But with our boss asking me to do it, I had no choice.

I looked at the storyboard. They had based the commercial on the Xerox ability to make copies that were as close to the original as possible. It was the early days of copiers and the business world was used to using ill-smelling mimeograph machines and duplicators that used special crinkly paper to copy something. But at the time, Xerox had the patent on copying onto ordinary paper so the copies were superior to anything else available.

Their storyboard told the story very graphically. It had the spokesman standing in front of two giant pieces of paper lying on the floor behind him, giant blowups of an original document and of a copy a Xerox machine had made of it.

He spoke of how faithful the Xerox copies were to the original. The commercial went along fine but I had to agree (silently) with our boss that the end was flat. It was just the standard "to learn more, contact your Xerox representative" call to action.

Our boss dismissed us with a "See what you can do, Don" and as we walked down the hall I apologized to my friends. But they understood that it wasn't my fault and assured me that our friendships weren't damaged.

But back sitting alone in my office I had to come up with some kind of "charming ending" my boss expected of me. I stared at my typewriter, out the window, down the hall, at my wall, then back at my typewriter. I repeated the ceremony over and over for what seemed like an eternity.

But suddenly an idea came to me: what if the copy was so close to the original that even the spokesman couldn't tell the difference?

Still standing before the two giant pieces of paper, near the end of the commercial he says,

MAN: Xerox makes copies so well that you can't tell the
     copy…
     HE POINTS TO THE PAPER ON THE LEFT
     THEN HESITATES, RECONSIDERING.
     You can't tell the copy…
     CHANGES HIS MIND AND POINTS TO THE
     PAPER ON THE RIGHT.
     from the original…
     POINTS TO THE PAPER ON THE LEFT AND IS
     NOW CONFUSED.
     er, uh…from the original
     CHANGES HIS MIND AGAIN AND CAN'T DECIDE
     WHICH ONE IS THE COPY.
     HOPELESSLY CONFUSED, HE SCRATCHES HIS
     HEAD AS THE COMMERCIAL ENDS.

It was an ending that made its point but did it with a smile. I
took my idea to the two fellows who had created the spot and they
liked it and then showed it to our boss. It worked. And in a month
the commercial aired on national television, complete with my
"charming ending."

There's an epilogue to the story. The commercial ended up
winning a major creative award but when they announced it at the
ceremony I refused to go up on stage with the two fellows who had
created the spot. It was theirs.

My satisfaction was that I had come up with a "charming
ending," a skill I had never known I had until that moment.

* * *

Coming up with an idea for a creative television commercial can
be difficult. But shooting the commercial to bring it to life can
sometimes be even more difficult. It was birthing a good
commercial idea that resulted in one of the most outrageous
excesses I ever saw in my years in advertising.

While I was working at Needham Harper & Steers in New

York, ARCO gasoline was one of our exciting accounts. The company had been formed from the merger of three oil companies and our agency had the task of introducing the newly-merged firm to the American public. Unfortunately I wasn't working on the account but the creative group that did created some excellent work.

One of the challenges they faced was to develop an ad campaign that spoke to the high level of care ARCO gave to its customers' cars. The slogan they came up with was "To Us Your Car is People."

Now the creative problem they had was how to illustrate the line graphically. Their solution was a dramatic television spot with a surprise ending. According to the storyboard, the final 10 seconds of the commercial started with an overhead shot looking down on a group of people that filled the frame. As the announcer voiced the line, the camera pulls back slowly revealing more and more people until finally, as the camera reaches its highest point, we discover that this seemingly aimless mass of people is in the shape of a car. It was a dramatic way to illustrate the "To Us Your Car is People" line. The client loved it and gave their approval to produce the commercial.

The agency producer responsible for bringing the spot to life was very excited at the prospect because, at the first production meeting, it was decided that the final shot, which had to be filmed from a helicopter, would be too expensive to shoot in the United States. Hiring that mass of people and the helicopter to film them would be less expensive if the commercial was done in Europe, probably France.

The prospect of producing a commercial in the south of France immediately went to the producer's head and, as they say, he 'Went Hollywood.' Assuming the persona of a big-time feature film producer, he let everyone within hearing distance know that he'd be going to France to shoot a commercial. He managed to drop it into every conversation he had, probably even to our cleaning people.

When he got to France he went even more big-time. Not concerned with any expense account limits, he stayed in the finest hotel and bought drinks and dinner not just for the clients who were there but also for the production people on his crew as well as the occasional stranger he wanted to impress.

But looming over everything was the reason he was there—the grand finale payoff shot of the "To us your car is people" line. Shooting from a helicopter can be difficult because helicopters are inherently unstable. And meeting the precise demands the storyboard called for was an especially difficult challenge. With the cameraman hanging out the side of the helicopter, the pilot had to hover over the small group of people then slowly lift straight up till it reached an altitude where the group of people was revealed to be in the shape of a car.

The day of the shoot, a couple of hours were spent positioning the dozens of extras so they formed the shape of a 30-foot car. But the producer suddenly faced a major problem. When he told the helicopter pilot what was required for the shot, the pilot stopped him cold. The shot the script called for was illegal, he said. There was no way he could fly his helicopter directly over a crowd of people and rise vertically over them. Any sudden loss of power or an unexpected shift in the wind could be disastrous.

But he had a possible solution. What he could do was to position his helicopter in the air slightly off to the side of the group and climb at a slight angle until the whole shape of the car was revealed. He assured them it would work fine. Moreover, it was legal and wouldn't endanger the dozens of extras in the shot.

The producer wasn't comfortable. Using his powers as a "big-time" American producer, he insisted on "riding the shot"— flying in the helicopter during a rehearsal to be sure the shot would work.

He climbed aboard, the pilot revved the rotor and they lifted off. Following his suggested plan, the pilot hovered 10 feet off the ground then climbed to the designated altitude to capture the car-shaped mass of people. When they landed, the producer had big grin on his face. "It works," he said. "Let's shoot it."

The cameraman climbed in replacing the producer and the helicopter lifted off. This was it. Because of time and budget constraints they had only one chance. With the camera rolling, the pilot flew the same profile up to the final altitude. The cameraman was satisfied and radioed back that they had the shot.

Today, a scene shot on film is shot simultaneously on video so the scene could be reviewed instantly. But in those days, the film had to be developed before a shot could be viewed. Not wanting to entrust the precious film to a French lab, the producer carried the exposed film with him on his flight back to New York and, when he arrived, messengered it to a New York processing lab.

The next day the lab delivered the crucial and ultra-expensive shot to the agency. With bated breath, the entire ARCO account group gathered in the screening room to see the result of the difficult labors of the producer and his production team.

The screening room lights went down and the film rolled. There was the mass of people milling about just like the storyboard pictured. But as the camera lifted up, something was wrong. Instead of moving straight up over the crowd, it was going at some weird angle. The small mass of people shown at the beginning grew into more and more people until the camera reached its final position revealing...a big mass of people. The shape that was revealed didn't look anything like a car. The pilot's modified flight path may have been safer for the people on the ground but it was disastrous for the people at the agency.

All the time, labor, travel and money spent on the climactic shot had been wasted. Instead of revealing a car-shaped group of people, they had spent upwards of $15,000 to show a small group of people turning into a large group of people.

The client was unhappy. The agency was embarrassed. And I was incredibly relieved that I wasn't working on the account.

* * *

"When you're creating advertising, there's no such thing as a bad idea."

When I was told that by one of my creative supervisors early in my career I laughed...silently, of course. Facing that blank page or computer screen, it seemed to me like we came up with plenty of bad ideas. I would dismiss nine out of ten headline ideas my partner and I would come up with, not even bothering to write them all down.

But as I matured creatively I started noticing that some of my best creative work, whether an ad, a TV spot or an outdoor billboard had started out as a silly or even stupid idea. But as I turned that silly or stupid idea around in my head it changed into a very unsilly and unstupid winning idea.

For many years, my creative partners and I had handled numerous and ultimately successful assignments by following the "no such thing as a bad idea" rule. We'd brainstorm—write down every idea we had, no matter how wild or way-out it was then reviewed them. It was always surprising—and satisfying—when we found an idea in the pile that we could bend and twist into a winner.

So I was very pleased when a major research firm asked me to join them as an advisor on one of their most successful services. They had developed a sophisticated form of brainstorming that was successful in coming up with ideas for innovative new products or services their client could offer.

These day-long sessions were always well attended. The client was generally represented by as many as three dozen people from their company, their ad agency and other advisors. They were divided up into groups of six or seven with a member of our research team—I was one of them—heading each group.

A key member of the research firm acted as a facilitator launching creative exercises designed to stimulate thinking by the groups. The exercises were fun, often funny, and every idea that was generated was written down on large pads. No editing. When an exercise was over, the sheets were put up on the wall. At the end of several hours, the walls were covered with dozens of sheets containing hundreds of ideas.

The client group was then thanked and dismissed. That's when our research team really went to work. We reviewed the ideas and began to find how some might be converted into positive, effective concepts the client could use.

A good example of how the process worked was when we travelled to a mid-western city to help a major newspaper. Their problem was that readership of their sports section had dropped significantly and both their subscriptions and newsstand sales had suffered. One of the hundreds of ideas that came out of the session seemed, like most of the ideas, ridiculous as well as useless. The idea was to print all the pictures in the sports section upside-down.

We chuckled at first but suddenly one of our group said those magic words, "Hey, wait a second..." His tone of voice said he was onto something.

"What if the photos in the section were difficult to read?"

Then someone added, "Why not print them so they needed those red-green glasses to see them?"

Someone else chimed in, "Why not have one photo in 3D so the reader needed glasses to get the effect?"

"What if that 3D photo was the basis for a contest with a major travel prize for the winner?"

In less than a minute, a dopey idea had been converted into a major marketing move.

The research firm wrote up its report that included among other ideas the 3D contest. The client loved the idea and a month or so later launched the idea. The response was immediate. Readership jumped for the duration of the contest and after it was over, there was the expected drop in readership. But it remained well above the level it had fallen to so the paper netted a healthy gain.

And it was all born from a once-dopey idea. Brainstorming had triumphed again.

* * *

That old creative muse can hit you on the head with her wand at the most unexpected times. You have to be ready to get bopped at any time. Once she even hit me while I was on a golf course.

When I left Foote Cone Belding/LA to start a new agency, our biggest account was Sunrise Company, a major developer of country club communities in the Palm Springs area. The newest community we were promoting was PGA West which our advertising had dubbed "The Western Home of American Golf" thanks to the use of the PGA name.

The grandest golf course there was the Stadium Course and they were eager to show it off to the golf world. We had watched it develop from a pile of desert sand to a championship course that was as beautiful as it was difficult. The executive in charge of developing the course told me that he had given course designer Pete Dye an unlimited budget and Pete had exceeded it. But it was worth the money because the course was as lovely to look at as it was to play.

One of the best ways to promote a golf course is to hold a major tournament there and the developers scored a coup by arranging to have the Skins Game played there on the Stadium Course. That would give both the course and PGA West national television coverage.

The Skins Game is a unique challenge to the pros and a unique way for them to make a lot of money. The rules were simple. A foursome of top professionals would play the course. Each hole had a reward known as a "skin." Each skin in the early holes was worth $25,000 and increased in value as the match progressed. The player who won a hole pocketed that money. If no one won the hole, the money was carried over to the next hole. If there was no winner on a series of consecutive holes, the skins added up and the reward to whoever finally won a hole could be substantial.

The excitement built as the day of the tournament approached. With four major pros competing for big money, a big crowd was expected. This would expose fans not just to the golf course but also to the homes at PGA West that our client wanted to sell.

In creating a newspaper ad to appear the week before the Skins Game, we decided to feature the most dramatic hole on the Stadium Course, the 17th.

It was an island green, totally surrounded by water other than a thin strip of land that allowed golfers access to the hole. In

The ad that helped bring attention to the challenging course our client, Sunrise Company ,wanted to promote. What happened when the Skins Game was played there brought more attention than we could ever have hoped for.

practicing on the hole a week before the event, I saw a lot of my golf balls drop into the water, never to be seen alive again.

The full-page ad we created featured a picture of the island green and sported the headline "Fantasy Island." We felt the headline worked because not only was it a good description of the island green itself but was also the name of a popular television show of the time.

On the day of the Skins Game, I was in the gallery watching Arnold Palmer, Jack Nicklaus, Fuzzy Zoeller and Lee Trevino compete. It was exciting watching the sport's greatest golfers playing for some of golf's greatest stakes.

On the back nine, the four tied hole after hole so the prize money for the first player to win a hole was building up. By the time they reached the 17th hole with its island green that we had featured in our ad, the prize money had built up to $175,000. As each of them hit off the tee, they avoided the water, their balls bouncing squarely on the green. Then Lee Trevino teed up his ball. He swung, his ball arced high over the water and landed on the green. But there was a difference. His ball rolled slowly toward the hole…and after a few heart-stopping seconds, dropped in. It was a hole-in-one!

An enormous scream erupted from the crowd. With that one stroke, Trevino had won $175,000. It was chaos. A hole-in-one was exciting enough but the huge reward he got for doing it made it even more exciting. I was also excited for another reason: that dramatic moment would focus even more attention on our client's property.

Walking to the final hole, I was thinking about ways to capitalize on Trevino's magic moment. Then it hit me. Why not take the same ad that had run two days earlier and, considering all the money Trevino had won on the hole, change the headline from "Fantasy Island" to "Treasure Island."

As soon as I got back to Los Angeles and my computer, I

rewrote the ad telling the story of Trevino's big win. The next morning I had our art director change the headline and copy and sent the revised ad to the *LA Times*. It ran the next day and we knew we had a winner. The first time the ad had run it had gotten good recognition. But this time the whole golf world was talking about it. So Lee Trevino wasn't the only big winner. Our client cashed in too.

* * *

When the Eisenhower Medical Center in the Palm Springs area opened an important new facility, they asked us to create a large billboard to announce it. This was the result.

* * *

In the late 1970's, BBDO/West had won an intense five-agency competition for the account of a company that produced hard drives and other peripheral products for computers. It had been a strange competition. The company had asked that the competing agencies present creative work in their presentation. To help us, they gave each a three-hour tour of their facility and in-depth briefing.

I was enthralled. Even then, several years before Apple made computers a universal must-have, I was a computer nut having received a build-it-yourself home computer kit from my wife as a wedding present a few years earlier. Part of it was probably my fascination with computers and part was just plain luck, but I came up with an idea for a campaign right in the middle of the client's facilities tour and briefing session.

Of course, I kept my idea to myself until we got back to the agency. Although I was excited about it, I figured the campaign was just a quick no-brainer that seemed good on the surface but had no depth. But I was wrong. Everyone agreed it was right on-target and we should go with it.

The trouble was that we couldn't make it look too easy to the client. Like a magician who blows a trick the first time or a gymnast who misses the bar, the end result is appreciated more if you have to work hard to get it. Or you appear to work hard. So while my creative team was bringing the campaign to life creating ads and commercials—which came to us as easily as the campaign itself—the account team called the client daily asking questions to make it appear as if we were searching hard for a campaign.

The presentation ran smoothly and was well-received and two days later we were awarded the account. We were especially pleased when the advertising director congratulated us. It was obvious to him that we had put in a lot of hard work and he really appreciated it.

All work should be that hard.

* * *

Good creative work rarely comes that easily. More often, a lot of work goes on before the writers and art directors of the creative department get to work on a product. That was the case when my agency, Needham Harper & Steers/New York was awarded Edge, a new shaving product that was dramatically different from its competition. Getting the assignment to create advertising for it sounded great to us…at first.

Most products appear to be "me-too" products. We usually had to work hard to create advertising that separated our client's coffee or beer or whiskey from their competition. But you could see that

Edge was different the second you tried it. Unlike all other shave products that came out of the can in the form of foam, Edge came out in the unique form of a green gel.

"Whoopee," we creative folk thought. We could show a product that people could instantly see was very different. But after our initial elation, we bumped into reality with some thoughts the public would probably think: "So what?" "Who cares?" "What's the big deal?"

That was what we faced when we were given the task of launching Edge. This was an important product launch for both our client, S.C. Johnson and for the agency. For Johnson, Edge would be the first personal grooming product they would introduce after decades of building their brand around household cleaning products like Johnson's Pledge and Johnson's Glo-Coat. For the agency it was our chance to shine because, until then, all Johnson assignments had gone to our Chicago office. This was the first job to go to our New York office. If we did well it could mean a chance for more Johnson business.

So we had to face that big "It's a gel. Who cares?" that we knew the public would ask. What was it about that difference that would convince the consumer to buy it? Before we could start creating advertising we had to turn to a powerful weapon in the marketing arsenal—consumer research.

There are many different tools in the research arsenal. The one our research department chose for Edge was a concept test. A concept test avoids one of the dangers researchers sometimes face—a humorous or clever ad or commercial may score well but the message doesn't sell well. People like the advertising but not necessarily the product. A concept test avoids that. There are no clever ads or commercials involved to win the person over. The subject is given a simple list of various product benefits and asked which of them appeals to him or her. No sexy, humorous or clever executions to influence them.

Our test was phrased very simply: "Because Edge comes out in the form of a gel..." and then we added a benefit. For example, "Because Edge comes out in the form of a gel it's less expensive." Or, "Because Edge comes out in the form of a gel you can shave faster." Some of the benefits in our list were real and some of them were imaginary. If an imaginary benefit won, of course we couldn't use it so we crossed our fingers that the winning benefit would be real.

When the results came in, we were floored. The benefit we had made up for the research and thought was least likely to be popular turned out to be the most popular by far: "Because Edge comes out in the form of the gel it's harder to cut yourself." We were very fortunate in that the claim was true. In speaking with the chemists who had developed Edge, they had talked about it having a low coefficient of friction. We had no idea what the heck they were talking about but the scientific fact was that having a low coefficient of friction helped the blade glide more smoothly and, in fact, made nicks and cuts less likely. So we had lucked out—the product actually was able to deliver on the promise that consumers were most interested in.

Armed with this valuable information, the Edge team was able to start creating advertising directed to the shavers' need. To capitalize on the gel's built-in cut-resistance, we recommended changing the name from plain old vanilla Edge Shave Gel to Edge Protective Shave. Then the team developed a slogan to make that benefit memorable: "Edge Protective Shave. To cut yourself you've almost got to be trying."

Then came the creative part of the project—creating a commercial to introduce Edge to the world.

We knew that the commercial had to be different from anything Johnson had ever done before. Their usual spots were of the happy-hands-at-home, female homemaker-oriented brand, hard on selling, short on freshness. Think of a Pledge furniture polish commercial—"...the table on the left is protected by Pledge while the table on the right is..." There's nothing wrong with them at all. They've made the Johnson family very wealthy. But Edge was a different product and at the agency we believed that, to have an impact, it had to break away from the usual Johnson style.

The commercial we developed was so different that it scared the client. It opened in a cowboy bunkhouse. A cowboy bursts in bellowing, "Who took my Edge?" He then goes to three cowboys and checks their faces. All of them are plastered with bloodied toilet paper patches covering cuts. He knows they didn't take his Edge.

Then he checks a fourth cowboy's face. It's smooth as a baby's bottom. "Give my Edge back," he demands. As the culprit hands the can to our hero, he asks, "How'd you know I took your Edge?"

The reply: "No nicks and no cuts on your face. It's a dead giveaway."

Then the final title over the Edge can: "Edge Protective Shave. To cut yourself you've almost got to be trying."

At the agency we loved it. It got the promise across with humor, a great marketing tool when it works.

But love wasn't the response we got when we presented the storyboard to the Johnson marketing director. It was so different from anything the company had ever done before that it scared the daylights out of him. It would never fly. "Crap," I recall was his description of it. He told us to go back to New York and give him a commercial he could use.

As we were sadly packing up to head back to the airport, his boss walked in—Sam Johnson, the "S" in S.C.Johnson. The marketing director told Johnson that we had brought them a crappy commercial and he had ordered us to return with something good that they could use.

But with a smile, Johnson said he was curious—he'd like to see the crappy commercial we had come up with. Quickly unpacking the storyboard, I presented the spot to him. When I finished, there was silence as we all turned and looked at Johnson. He had a big grin on his face. He liked it and immediately approved it for production and a few weeks later we were sitting in a California casting office looking for just the right cowboy.

Casting and shooting the commercial was a joy that was described earlier. But the real joys were yet to come. The first came when we screened the finished commercial to Mr. Johnson at Johnson's Wisconsin headquarters. He liked it so much that he insisted we show it to all the employees. So we spent the rest of the day screening it numerous times for dozens of smiling employees.

The next joy was when Johnson used our commercial to introduce Edge in a single city test market. Within three weeks, Edge was outselling the market-leading shave product, Gillette Foamy. Armed with that successful test, they rolled out Edge nationally and S.C. Johnson had a hit on their hands. Their foray into a whole new category, personal grooming, was a success. A new brand was born.

And our ad agency was the obstetrician.

* * *

My agency, Needham Harper & Steers/New York, was helpful in another birth. But this was not just of a new product—it was the birth of an invention that changed the way the world does business.

During a meeting at Xerox headquarters in Rochester in 1970, the marketing director unexpectedly gave each of us a Non-Disclosure Agreement to sign. Once we signed it, we were legally prevented from revealing to anyone what he was about to show us. Our client said nothing about the secret he was about to reveal but, from the sly smile on his face, we knew it had to be good.

He led us down the hall to a room with a locked door and a sign that read, "Project Redeye." Unlocking the door, he ushered us into a small windowless room. On the table in the center was a small object the size of a portable sewing machine with a telephone dial at one end and telephone cables running from it into the wall.

Without preamble, he took a typed page from the table and wrapped it around the cylinder of the machine. After dialing a number, he pressed a button. The cylinder began spinning and a tiny red light began scanning slowly across the paper as it spun.

"Okay, we give up. What's happening?" one of our team asked.

"I'm sending this memo to an office in Los Angeles."

"Over the phone?"

"Over the phone," he responded, a smile splitting his face as he enjoyed our combination of puzzlement and awe.

He explained that, as the machine scanned the document, it converted each light and dark point it saw into sound signals that it sent over the phone to a matching machine at the other end. There its mate reconverted the sounds it received back into a copy of the sending document. The time to scan and send a page? Six minutes.

We were really impressed. Sending a document anywhere in the world via telephone was unheard of. What we witnessed that day in that small room was the birth of a machine Xerox called the Telecopier. But in a few years it would be known by another name—the fax machine. And it would revolutionize the way the world does business.

We were responsible for introducing this new technology to the world. The first ad one of our teams created for the machine not only won readers, it won several major advertising awards. Capitalizing on the ease and speed of sending documents anywhere via the telephone, the ad featured a pencil drawing of an ancient biplane. The headline: "Coast to Coast in 6 Minutes."

* * *

In print advertising we usually think of creativity in terms of clever words and/or graphics. But sometimes you can be creative by delivering the client's message in a unique way. That was certainly the case with several of the clients I served.

When I was a partner in my own agency, we were very pleased when Absolut Vodka asked us to help them. They had been running an award-winning series of clever ads, all adhering to the same strict format—an Absolut bottle shown in some unique way with a two-word headline at the bottom that described the bottle.

Their charge to us was to do an Absolut ad that commemorated Earth Day. With the calibre of the ads in their campaign and the major agencies that had created them, we knew they were expecting us to do something memorable. It was a big challenge.

Our solution: a picture of an Absolut bottle made up of

These two Absolut Vodka ads we did were unique, each
containing something completely unexpected.

illustrations of wildflowers with a headline that read "Absolut Spring." But the element that hit the ball out of the park was an actual packet of wildflower seeds glued onto the ad in every magazine it appeared. It was so successful that Absolut chose the ad for the coveted cover of their annual calendar.

With the success of our "Absolut Spring" ad, the client asked us to do another ad to show their concern for the environment.

To satisfy their request, we developed an ad that, like our wildflower seed packet, held a surprise—a button that the reader pressed to hear a save-the-environment message from Absolut.

* * *

Another ad delivery method we used was actually not very new—3D. We had grown up looking through View-Master viewers at vivid three-dimensional pictures of everything from Jack and Jill dolls to awe-inspiring views of the Grand Canyon. But, as far as we knew, 3D technology had never been used in magazine advertising.

Through a contact at Toyota we proposed doing an ad for them that was bound into a magazine along with a cardboard 3D viewer that would feature a picture of one of their cars. They

agreed and we developed an ad for their Corolla that would appear along with a 3D viewer. The viewer contained a vivid three-dimensional photo of their new Corolla on San Francisco's steep, winding Lombard Street. Before the ad appeared, management previewed it to dealers at a national Toyota convention. It was a rousing success and, according to Toyota management, really excited the dealers.

The combination of the appeal of this 3D viewer to readers and the way it fired up the dealers, really worked—sales of the Corolla were 60 percent higher than the same period the previous year.

The sales action that our Toyota 3D ad brought didn't go unnoticed by the industry and not long afterwards we got an assignment from General Motors to do a 3D ad. The difference with this one was that our viewer not only showed a 3D beauty shot of the car but was shaped like it as well.

This 3D viewer we created for General Motors had an added extra — it was shaped like the SUV it promoted.

Again, using 3D creatively paid off. Like with Toyota, we got feedback that both the dealers and the public were turned on by it. The extra expense it had cost the client was well worth it.

* * *

Creativity can take a lot of different forms. On a commercial shoot in Las Vegas I learned just how different those forms could be.

We had created a series of commercials designed to run during the winter in Western Airlines' colder cities, tempting people to fly Western to their warm weather cities. One of the most desirable of those cities was Las Vegas so it was only natural that we build a commercial around it.

Predictably, the spot called for showgirls and so, during a pre-production visit to Las Vegas, our producer, Jim Baier, approached several shows to see if they were interested in participating in the commercials. The manager of one of the major shows was willing to let us use their girls and their lavish costumes if we publicized their show in our spot. Always eager to sell out for a good cause, I rewrote the spot to show our hero walking past a big Las Vegas Strip sign advertising the show.

Two weeks later we were back in Vegas with our entire crew, fifteen strong, ready and eager to shoot the commercial. But when our producer called the manager of the show, he was stunned. The manager had changed his mind. Period. No explanation, no apology, no recourse. We couldn't use his show's famous name or any of the show's fabulous costumes.

We were in trouble. This spot was one of six we were scheduled to shoot across the country. Our production schedule was precisely timed and if one spot fell out of bed the entire schedule behind it was damaged. Besides adding thousands of dollars to the budget, it would mean we would probably miss the date the commercials were scheduled to begin airing. We had to shoot. Somehow.

The day before the shoot, our production coordinator, Janice Flating, spoke to the dance captain of the showgirls. The eight girls our script called for were happy to appear in our spot. But they had nothing to wear. We were scheduled to start shooting at eight the next morning and at four in the afternoon Jim Baier had a not-so-brilliant idea—*we* would make the costumes.

Janice and her assistant commandeered our production van and disappeared. With our stress levels skyrocketing, no one in our four-person agency team felt like eating an elaborate dinner so we had light suppers sent up to one of the rooms where we munched disconsolately. Just as were finishing, in walked Janice.

"Well, this is them," she announced, reaching into a big shopping bag. From its depths she pulled her prizes...eight one-piece bathing suits. There was a collective groan.

"They're not going to cut it, Janice," Jim warned. Janice smiled and, a moment later, in walked a parade of bellhops. They carried a hoard of boxes that they deposited on the beds. Janice walked over and dramatically opened the boxes one by one as if showing off the treasures of the Orient. Actually, they contained the treasures of Las Vegas—sequins, feathers, boas, plastic baubles and dangly things. Opening a bag filled with sewing needles and thread, she announced, "Let's get to work."

And so it was that two talented wardrobe women and four very inept advertising men sat down and began creating, under Janice's direction, eight glamorous showgirl costumes. Lou Goldberg, our art director, turned out to be a superb sewer. Jim, his omnipresent pipe gritted firmly in his teeth, hardly got past threading his first needle when he gave up sewing and began gluing things instead.

We sewed sequins and beads in patterns across the face of the suits. We added borders of dangly things. We edged some outfits top and bottom with colored boas. We converted shower caps to showgirl headdresses with sequins and peacock feathers (artificial, in keeping with the Las Vegas taste code.) It was extremely slow work but the combination of our esprit de corps and room service wine kept us going and, just as the clock struck four a.m., Janice added the final touch to the final costume. We had done it! If you looked closely you could see all the mistakes but in Las Vegas you were better off not looking closely at anything anyway.

We all grabbed a few hours of sleep and at 8 a.m. were down in the casino as our eight showgirls came in and looked at their costumes. Besides being beautiful, the girls were great. They laughed at our adventure and even harder at the outfits. They had to be donned very carefully. As one of the girls slipped into one of our original creations, a row of poorly sewn beads flew off and went cascading like runaway ball bearings across the stage. Sequins fluttered to the ground like colored snowflakes. But we knew the costumes were disposable. They just had to hold up through two hours of filming.

We had to do a fair amount of pinning and gluing as we shot but they made it. When we saw the dailies the next day, we were thrilled. Our impromptu creativity had paid off. They may have looked like hell in person but on film you couldn't tell our artificial schlock costumes from the genuine schlock costumes of Las Vegas.

* * *

In ranking the types of creative assignments I enjoyed the most, creating brochures was pretty far down the list. But there were exceptions and one brochure assignment I got stood out both from the challenge it represented and from the amazing result it got.

In the agency I formed when I left the big agency world, one of our clients was a developer of country club communities in Southern California. We had helped him successfully launch a number of his communities but this assignment he gave us was unique.

He owned a large ranch in the Santa Ynez Valley north of Los Angeles that he wanted to sell and asked us to create a sales brochure. When we visited the ranch we knew it couldn't be an ordinary brochure because this was no ordinary property. It was beautiful, stretching out over 2,700 acres, featuring a magnificent central home, a luxurious guesthouse, a beautiful lake along with numerous other lavish features. The asking price was equally lavish—over $30 million.

A rare property like this deserved a rare brochure. The one we developed we believed was worthy of the property. It measured some 16 x 30 inches, contained over thirty glossy pages filled with rich color pictures and came with a simulated leather cover embossed with the ranch logo.

The property went up for sale and a number of prospective buyers, hopefully enticed by our brochure, visited it. And then one day we received a phone call. The property had been sold.

The new owner took over the ranch and made a number of

changes adding, among other things, an amusement park and a zoo. One of the changes was the new name he gave it: Neverland.

Our brochure had helped draw the interest—and ultimately the investment—of Michael Jackson.

This real estate brochure we created helped make a sale that made headlines across the country...and around the world.

∞ 8 ∞

FASCINATING FOLK

I've never known what it was about advertising that attracted so many interesting people but my career has been full of them.

Some were good guys and gals, some were baddies. But hero or villain, they were a memorable collection of people that made my years in the business interesting, fun, stressful, rewarding, frustrating, educational, painful...you pick the adjective and it will fit. All in all, it made my choice of profession a good one for me.

Herewith a sampling of the people I encountered. Interesting? You be the judge.

From the day modern advertising was born, there frequently has been a schism between the copywriter-art director teams of the creative department and the account executives and account supervisors who are the chief link between the agency and its clients. This perennial civil war is based on two premises. Account people often think of creative people as temperamental prima donnas. Creative people sometimes think that account folk don't fight hard enough to sell their work and consider them to be just "messenger boys" or, worse yet, "empty suits." They're both inaccurate and unfair generalizations but from time to time there's some truth on either side.

There was my copywriter who went ballistic when the account executive returned from a meeting with a client and told her the client had changed two words in her ad.

Or the account executive who could change his mind to agree with a client so quickly that my boss swore that at one meeting the man's hair was parted on the left and three seconds after the client voiced an opinion his hair was parted on the right.

But the account person who lived up to every creative person's nightmares come true was one I worked with at Needham Harper & Steers in New York. Bob was handsome with chiseled features, a Roman nose, salt and pepper hair and a briar pipe constantly jutting from his strong jaw. He would have been the dream of the casting director of *Mad Men* if they were looking for a slick, smarmy businessman. As an account supervisor, he was responsible for overseeing relations with his clients and coordinating the various aspects of the agency's responsibilities on the account like media, creative and research.

One of the people he worked with estimated that his ego was slightly larger than Cincinnati. And he proved it when we moved to new quarters on Third Avenue. The first thing he did was to count the number of ceiling tiles in his office. When he found that he had one row less than another account executive, solid evidence that his office was smaller by ten inches, he stormed into the chairman's office and complained. But to no avail. The offices had been assigned. He pouted for weeks.

In another outrage, Bob was hiring a secretary. When he found one he was interested in, he informed her that he had a very important position and it was vital that his secretary be a good representative of his lofty stature. So he insisted that they go to her apartment and that she give him a fashion show of her wardrobe to be sure she represented his position adequately. She did, he got his fashion show and he got away with it. Today his demand alone would have launched a lawsuit as large as his ego.

I got involved with him only once, but that was enough. One of his clients was Italian Lines, a cruise ship line owned and operated by the Italian government. That wasn't one of my regular accounts but when the creative team that usually handled the account was busy, they called on me and my team to develop a TV commercial.

After learning more about the unique features the Italian Line offered, in a few days we created a storyboard for a 30-second spot. We showed our storyboard to the creative director and after we made a few of his suggested changes, he approved it enthusiastically. The next step was to show the storyboard to Bob.

He hated it. He was firm, almost angry. No way would he allow me to show it to the client. When I reported his response to the creative director, he saw red. Creative work, he said, was judged by the creative department and I was to present the storyboard to the client and to hell with Bob.

At the client meeting it was obvious to us, if not to the client, that Bob wasn't happy. However he had no choice but to let me stand up and present the storyboard. As I began explaining the first of the twelve frames, the client started smiling almost immediately. By the time I reached the fourth frame, the client was wearing a full grin. It was going really well. Bob saw this and suddenly leaped out of his seat, grabbed the storyboard from my hands and presented the rest of the spot to the client himself.

Our Italian client, of course, responded to the big finish of the commercial with a genuine "Bravo!" Bob bowed modestly, basking in the glory of our commercial that he had hated so vehemently moments earlier.

The upshot? Some loud nasty words with Bob after the client left, first a lot from me and later, more from the creative director. But the commercial was produced and was well-received. And to the client, Bob was a hero. Again, justice was unserved and he got away with it.

But Bob's biggest outrage was yet to come. The agency had developed a big radio campaign for another of his clients. The budget for buying airtime to run the commercials was big and spread over some two dozen radio stations across the country. While the media department was purchasing the airtime, someone in the agency got a phone call from one of the stations. A group of the stations, he said, had gotten together and decided to brave Bob's wrath and rat him out. He had sent out the word that if they wanted to get the business from his account, they would have to kick back a percentage of their income to him. When word got to the agency's management, they, like everyone else, were more than furious.

But they didn't do anything about it for a good, if not proper, reason: Bob was splitting his take with the client's advertising director and if the agency blew the whistle, the ad director would fire us. Bob was ordered to return his portion of the swag to the stations but nothing was said to the ad director. The agency kept the account and, unfortunately, lost a certain amount of self-respect.

* * *

One film assignment I got led me to meet with one of the most colorful—and bizarre—people I ever worked with.

Because of the many commercials I had written, I had worked with a number of commercial production houses—companies that, via film or tape, brought my storyboards to life. It was through one of these production houses that I got a very interesting assignment.

The director I had worked with at one of the major production houses asked me if I was interested in writing and directing a documentary film about the Flying Doctors, or as it's known in Mexico, Los Médicos Valadores. One weekend a month, member doctors and dentists fly their planes from southern California airports to Mexican villages bringing medical aid to people who often have no other access to modern medicine. It sounded like an interesting assignment and I readily agreed. That "yes" led me to meet that ultra-colorful, one-in-a-million man.

Before writing the script, I had to learn about the organization so I asked to fly on one of the group's monthly weekend missions. I was assigned to fly with Doctor Burke. I was really excited about the assignment. As a pilot myself, I was being paid to do something that I love and, on top of that, the subject I was researching was interesting. And as I soon found out, Doctor Burke was to make it a lot more interesting.

He was successful both as a doctor and a businessman. Part of the evidence of that success was sitting in front of a hangar at Long Beach airport when we walked out to start our mission to Mexico—a shiny white twin-engine six passenger Cessna. It was an exquisite aircraft—expensive to buy and expensive to fly. Five of us—Dr. Burke, another doctor, two nurses and myself—climbed aboard.

As soon as we lifted off the runway I could tell he was a good pilot, calm and confident. My adventure had begun. I didn't know that the trip would arm me with stories about him I would tell for many years to come...but could never use in my film.

Doctor Burke had an instrument rating, meaning he was licensed to fly in bad weather and at night solely by reference to instruments. But that didn't matter because, instrument rating or not, it was illegal to fly at night in Mexico. As we flew south toward Mexico, the sun was setting. But that didn't seem to bother him. When I asked him about it, he shrugged his shoulders. As I was to soon learn, nothing ruffled him.

Our destination was a small airport in a town in Baja California a hundred miles south of the border. As we flew illegally through the Mexican night, Doctor Burke was unconcerned. When we reached the airport, he flew a pass over the runway at about 200 feet. When I asked him why, he explained quite seriously that before we landed he wanted to chase off any stray cows that might be on the runway.

As we made the final turn toward the runway to land, a pair of headlights lit up at the far end of the runway.

"Oh, shit. Federales," Burke said ominously. As we touched down, he yelled to us, "Quick. Give me all your cash." The Mexican national police had a reputation for playing hardball with tourists. And, by flying at night we were all criminal tourists. They could do anything they wanted including confiscating the plane and throwing us in jail. Fortunately, the Federales had another reputation—being very amenable to *la mordita*, the bribe.

We each reached into our pockets and pulled out all the money we had and gave it to Burke as he braked the plane to a stop. When we opened the door and dropped the stairway, the Federales were standing there glowering menacingly with their machine guns cocked and, we were sure, very loaded. Burke got up from his pilot's seat, the stack of money in his back pocket, and moved to the door. When the first policeman saw him, the expression on the man's face instantly changed from anger to rapture.

"Senor Doctor Burke," he exclaimed. The faces on all three policemen were suddenly wreathed with smiles. As Burke descended the stairs, each of the men took his hand and shook it unmercifully.

They were in total awe. Doctor Burke was their idol. As he explained later, he had helped each of the men's families in some sort of health crisis and he was a hero in their eyes.

As Burke gave us our money back, the police ran to their car. He taxied the plane behind them as they led us to a parking spot on the ramp and helped us tie it down. They promised to guard it carefully, no small promise when you realize that the electronics on the plane alone were probably worth over $20,000. And best of all, we were honored by a luxurious ride to our hotel in a police van. It sure beat a ride to the local jail in a paddy wagon.

The next day we flew to a small village in the interior along with five other private planes carrying doctors, dentists and volunteers. The villagers viewed their visitors as gods and dozens of them waited patiently in the town square for their turn to be treated. The conditions were often crude but as sanitary as possible. A six-year-old little girl received the first dental examination of her life. A farmer received antibiotics for an infection that threatened to blind him.

There was very little privacy but no one seemed to care. In the square, the villagers watched as a doctor burned a skin cancer off the neck of a man using a soldering iron that had been heated over a nearby fire. A local anesthetic had made it painless for the man and when it was over the villagers let out a loud cheer for the doctor.

Dr. Burke saw at least two dozen patients before it was time to leave. The gratitude, the grasping hands and the tears of many of the villagers spoke of how precious the flying doctors' gifts were for them. I was very moved by their emotion and gained confidence that I could write a script for the film that would move audiences.

We flew back to the same airport where we had landed the night before and were again welcomed by the same Federales who had stood proudly at attention when we exited Dr. Burke's plane. When the good doctor was about to call the hotel to send a van for us, the police insisted. They again drove us proudly to the hotel in their police van.

Ordinarily the doctors would fly home the day after delivering their medical services. But Dr. Burke said he'd rather stay over an extra day. The weather was great and I had brought my bathing suit so was in no hurry. I woke up the next day and had a lovely breakfast but Dr. Burke was nowhere to be seen at the hotel. Our party spent the day reading, lounging at the pool and drinking a daiquiri or two.

We first saw Dr. Burke when he joined us for dinner. He didn't volunteer where he had spent the day and nobody ventured to ask him. After dinner we retired to the poolside bar and gradually the other members of our party retired. Finally, Dr. Burke and I were alone. By that time I had had enough wine to ask what was apparently unaskable. "Okay," I asked. "I give up. Where were you today?" His Cheshire Cat smile told me that, if he confessed, it was going to be a good one. And it was.

It seems that the woman who managed the hotel and Dr. Burke had once been lovers. But now unfortunately, she was married and lived with her husband in a cottage on the hotel grounds. If the two former lovers wanted privacy it would be pretty hard to lose the husband…unless you were Dr. Burke.

That morning he had casually asked the husband if he had ever seen the hotel property from the air. The husband had not so Dr. Burke invited him to take a personal aerial tour of the area. In 15 minutes Dr. Burke and the husband were climbing into the clear blue Mexican sky.

As he related it to me, Burke made the flight very exciting for the husband. First he climbed to 1,000 feet and flew over the area giving the husband a beautiful view of the hotel and its surrounding property. Then he suddenly banked sharply and dove straight at the hotel, leveled off less than 100 feet over the roof and buzzed the hotel grounds. When he was out over the water, he banked sharply again making several high speed turns. Pulling up to gain altitude, he performed a few moderate aerobatics and briefly flew upside-down.

Finally, the husband raised his hand. According to Burke, he was as green as the hotel's rich lawn. He had to get back on the ground or he was going to be sick in the plane.

As Burke landed the plane and rolled to a stop, he was terribly apologetic to the husband. He hadn't realized, he said, how his flying was affecting the husband. Burke assisted him back to his cottage and with profuse apologies, gave the husband two pills to help him relax and to settle his stomach. The husband was somewhat embarrassed and grateful for the doctor's kindness.

As he related the story to me, a sly smile began to creep on the good doctor's face. The pills he had given the husband had nothing to do with settling stomachs. They were actually powerful sleeping pills. Two of them were guaranteed to keep the husband asleep for at least seven hours. That gave the doctor and his former lover plenty of time to renew their lusty relationship. The two of them had emerged from the doctor's room only 10 minutes before dinner.

But the final chapter of my long weekend with Dr. Burke and the flying doctors was still to come. We took off late the next afternoon and by the time we approached Long Beach airport it was dark. As we were about to enter the landing pattern, Dr. Burke asked me if I would sit in the copilot's right-hand seat. He knew I was a pilot and said he'd like some help on the landing. What kind of help could I give an instrument-rated pilot with tens of thousands of hours of flying time?

As we made the first of two left hand turns towards the runway he said, "Don, call out the altitudes." Puzzled, I called out every hundred feet as we descended to the runway. As we dropped through 400 feet above the runway, I saw that we were descending a little rapidly so I told him.

"Thanks," he said as he added a little power to slow the descent. I continued calling out altitudes until we touched down. The landing was a little harder than usual but still quite safe.

As we taxied off the runway towards the ramp I was curious. "I was happy to help but why did you need me to call out altitudes?"

"Well, Don," he replied. "I forgot my glasses at the hotel and, to tell the truth, I couldn't see a damn thing for the whole flight."

That was a piece of information I was happy to receive after we landed, not before.

After three less adventurous trips with other members of the Flying Doctors, I wrote a script that the producers liked. But, as happens in the film world, the financing they had counted on didn't come through and the film was never produced.

But I've never had a moment of regret. Spending a weekend with the once-in-a lifetime Doctor Burke had made the effort more than worthwhile.

* * *

It was on one of my New York-to-California commercial shoots that I worked with one of funniest people I ever met.

On a film shoot, the second most important crewmember besides the director is the assistant director. The A.D. is responsible for making every one of the director's wishes come true. The cast, the extras, the food, the lighting, the props, the crew—he or she sees to it that the people responsible for every element of the production do their jobs and everything is ready and right when the director needs them. It's a tough job and I never met an A.D. who wasn't sharp and tough. But the one I remember best was sharp, tough and funny.

The time was the early '70's but Tommy was a poster boy for the '60s…long, stringy hair, droopy Fu Manchu mustache and tie-dye tops. But what really confirmed him as a 60's guy was when we met him for the first time the faint aroma of marijuana wafted around him. The director had worked with him before and told us that he was good…so good, in fact, that when the Rolling Stones played Los Angeles, he was their "nanny." He'd be responsible for getting them whatever their hearts desired…and, as he told us, it was a long and very interesting list.

But it wasn't just his efficiency that kept him in demand. It was his sense of humor. Our commercial called for an outdoor location and he recommended a site a half hour north of Los Angeles. While we were driving the freeway to check it out, he told us about a sideline he had—he had a grip truck he rented out. On a location shoot, a grip truck is a valuable piece of equipment. It carries the lighting, stands, tools and other equipment needed on a shoot. But besides having to have all the equipment on board, it was vital that it was all organized immaculately so that any piece of equipment that was needed, from a huge light to a roll of tape, could be accessed as quickly and as easily as possible. When a location shoot is costing over $100,000 a day, a five-minute delay searching for a piece of equipment on the grip truck is expensive.

Enroute to our location, Tommy pitched us hard to use his grip truck the next time we came to California for a shoot. As he was winding up his pitch, he said, "You couldn't find a better-equipped, more organized grip truck in the business."

Just then an old pickup truck rolled onto the freeway. Huge piles of crap—palm leaves, an oil drum and assorted junk littered the truck bed. In the middle of it were two stacks of old rubber tires and on the top of them was a Latino man who was bouncing up and down, frantically trying to keep from being catapulted over the side onto the freeway each time the truck hit an imperfection in the roadbed.

Without skipping a beat, Tommy said, "What a coincidence. There's our truck now."

He was just as funny the rest of the day as well as the day of the shoot. His humor offset the often-intense pressures of filming and I silently vowed to use Tommy on a future shoot.

But I never had occasion to use him again. I regret it to this day.

* * *

Art Guerrero's greatest skill was slipping on banana peels. He was an excellent copywriter at BBDO and I could always count on him to turn in excellent work. But his misadventures outside the office were legend and brought big smiles to many of our early morning coffee klaatches. If someone said "Did you hear what happened to Guerrero yesterday....?" we knew we were in for a good story.

One time he came to the office upset and told one of his fellow copywriters that his car had been stolen while he was at lunch at a restaurant in Hollywood. He had reported it stolen and had taken a cab to the office.

His friend asked him where he had parked the car. When Art told him it was on Cherokee Street off Hollywood Boulevard, his friend grinned. "Your car wasn't stolen, Art. It was towed. That street is a No Parking zone on Thursdays."

With that, Art moaned, smacked his forehead and looked up the number of the police auto impound garage. He gave them the make of his car and the license plate and, sure enough, his car was sitting in their garage. His friend dropped him off at the garage .

His parking was more than just illegal. It was costly. He had to pay a fine for violating the parking rule, pay for the tow to the impound garage and pay for a minimum of two hours storage in the garage. The bill was upwards of $200.

But the best/worst was yet to come. After he had paid the bill for his car, as Art drove it down Hollywood Boulevard, he was stopped and hauled over to the side by a police cruiser flashing its red and green roof lights. With a cry of "Get out and get on the ground," the officers did a full felony stop complete with drawn guns. As he lay on the ground with his hands cuffed behind his back, Art realized why he was there: he had failed to report that he had recovered his car.

The police had stopped him severely for a good reason: they thought he was driving a stolen car.

* * *

Another Art-ful event occurred when Art arrived at his home in one of Los Angeles' many canyons. As he exited his car, he saw and heard an odd sight: a cow was tied to the railing of his porch. And around the cow's neck hung a large red ribbon. The cow was obviously unhappy, mooing loudly, her moos echoing through the canyon.

Art's friends had played a practical joke on him. But as he approached the animal, what he saw wasn't very funny. Stapled to the ribbon was a summons for disturbing the peace. His gift cow had been there for a while and had been mooing unhappily and bothering his neighbors. They finally had had enough and had called the police.

With the still-mooing cow and the expensive summons, Art was understandably upset. Unable to stop the cow's mooing and worried that the continuing noise would draw the police again, he untied the cow and led her inside his living room. It wasn't a good decision. The cow showed her extreme displeasure by relieving herself on Art's once-lovely carpet.

Ultimately his friends couldn't resist and called him to find out how he did with the joke. Art's anger at discovering the cow brought gales of laughter from his friends. But that was nothing compared to the typhoons of laughter when he told them of his summons and how the cow had shown her displeasure on his carpet.

But they were good friends and good sports and ultimately chipped in to help pay for his summons and the carpet cleaning. It was another Art adventure with a somewhat happy ending.

* * *

Art's unique adventures didn't end when he passed away at an unfortunately young age. At his memorial service, his friends—including myself—told story after story of his wonderful adventures. Even though we all missed him, we smiled and even laughed, unusual for a memorial service. But Art's ultimate story was saved for last.

Art had been cremated and a dear friend of his had volunteered to go to the crematorium to pick up his ashes and take them to the interment service. At our memorial service she told us the story.

She had put the urn on her passenger seat and belted it in. When she got on the freeway she saw that traffic was virtually stopped. Looking at her watch, she knew that she would be terribly late for the service so, making an instant decision, she made her way onto the diamond lane where there was virtually no traffic. She told us that not 10 seconds later there were flashing lights behind her and a highway patrolman had her pull over.

"You know ma'am, you're supposed to have at least two people in the car to drive in this lane."

The combination of being late and then being pulled over upset her. Then suddenly she realized something.

"But officer, there *are* two people in this car."

The officer's eyes followed her as she gestured to the urn on the seat next to her.

She looked up at him. "He was my friend."

She explained why she had chosen to go into the diamond lane despite the risk.

The officer looked at her closely for a moment, then closed his notepad and said, "Follow me, ma'am."

With her police escort, she told us, she arrived at the memorial park five minutes ahead of schedule.

Art Guerrero had done it again. For the last time.

* * *

Losing an account can often be difficult, especially if the agency has produced good work that has been successful in selling the client's product. In one case, the person most responsible for a lot of the good work the agency had done was also responsible for torpedoing a major account.

The man was a principal of an agency and had built a reputation as a creative genius. Unfortunately, he had also built a reputation for his hot head and foul temper. The client, a major national advertiser, showed great patience, thanks to the award- and sales-winning work of the agency, much of it created by him.

But there were limits. And one day he reached them. It all took place in the client's august, mahogany-paneled conference room.

The creative man was presenting layouts for a series of new ads to a group of executives and it wasn't going well. After several ads in a row met with a cool reception, he picked up the next one, looked at it without showing it to his audience and said, "If you didn't like the last one, you probably wouldn't like this one either." And he dropped it on the floor. His anger building, he picked up another.

"And if you didn't like those, you're really going to hate this one," and, without showing it, threw it over his shoulder.

"And you're really going to despise this one," tossing another ad across the room. Then, taking the remaining pile of ads, he threw them in the air and, as they slowly settled down onto the conference room floor, stormed out of the room.

As he exited, his presentation was strewn all around the boardroom along with whatever remained of his agency-client relationship.

* * *

It's only natural that scattered among the many people I dealt with in the business there were some villains.

Advertising can be a stressful business. Whether it was looking at a tight deadline, having to justify a multimillion dollar media budget to a client or a facing an extremely blank piece of paper or computer screen waiting for me to fill it with a brilliant idea, stress lay in wait constantly. What I didn't need was a client or coworker to make it even more stressful. But occasionally these bad guys were there in all their gory glory.

One of the worst villains I ever encountered was actually a fellow employee in one of the agencies I worked at. What made it even worse was that I had to report to him. That made his villainy even more painful.

The pain that was to come started innocently enough. On my first day of work he was briefing me on the various clients I would be responsible for. One of them, he told me, was annoying him enormously. The client, the marketing director for a major bank, would call him constantly with demands and questions. He said to me, "The day he calls you, Don, instead of me you will have earned your entire year's salary."

I met the client and we appeared to get along. He was not a warm and cuddly person and could be very critical at times but we seemed to be building a good relationship. Then one day, about a month after I started working on his account, instead of calling my boss with a problem, he called me. I assured him I would handle it.

The moment I hung up, I leapt excitedly out of my chair and walked quickly down the hall to my boss's office. I walked in and with a proud smile on my face, announced, "I did it. Just what you wanted—instead of calling you with a problem he just called me."

I was surprised by my boss's reaction. Based on what he had said in his initial briefing to me, I had expected some sort of joy at the news that I had lifted the burden of the client off his shoulders. But instead, I received a very dull, flat, unsmiling, "Good."

Instead of enjoying the fact that I had won the difficult client's confidence, it bothered him. And he never forgave me.

Apparently, the fact that since I had arrived at the agency I had gained a measure of respect from our clients and from my employees upset him. He resented it and gradually his resentment toward me grew. My meetings with him were growing more and more chilly as time passed.

One day, after he had sat in on a meeting I had held with my creative teams, one of my art directors came into my office. She seemed reluctant to reveal what she had to say but apparently it was too much for her to keep to herself.

"After you left the meeting, Don" she said, "he made some pretty sarcastic comments about you."

I didn't react overtly but it registered with me. I had felt negative vibrations coming from him but they seemed vague and hard to pin down. I made light of it to her but not to myself. From then on, I was more aware that something was going on that I didn't like.

At a recording session for a radio commercial I had written, he said things out of my earshot that led people to glance at me. He did something similar while we were shooting a television commercial that appeared to generate some laughter...at my expense, no doubt.

I finally had had enough. One day I walked into his office and said, "Somebody in this agency is talking about me behind my back."

He looked at me from across the office as anger registered on his face and he moved towards me with his fists clenched. My Brooklyn background kicked in and in an instant I was ready to defend myself. When he saw that I wasn't going to give him a free shot at me—and apparently realizing that what he was about to do was incredibly stupid—he spun around, ran to the door of his office and, with his cowboy-booted foot, kicked a giant hole in it.

* * *

I left the agency not long after that to start my own agency. We were quite successful and about a year later at an advertising industry function I showed up driving a brand-new Porsche. Apparently word of my visible success reached him as I entered the building. And it obviously bothered him. With a big smile on my face, I approached him with my hand extended. He shook it with a smile so forced I thought his cheeks would crack.

As a wise man once said, "Success is the best revenge."

A few years later, he left the agency to form a new agency. Apparently he was not going to be missed. When the news broke that he was leaving, several people in the creative department tore reams of colored paper into confetti and skipped up and down the aisles of the agency gaily strewing the confetti and happily chanting, "Ding Dong, the Witch is Dead."

* * *

Steal my car. Steal my wallet. Steal my watch. All bad. But as a creative person, the worst things you can steal are my ideas. My ideas got me jobs, got me dollars, built my reputation, and, as with any creative person, were a singular source of pride.

While I worked at Cunningham and Walsh Advertising in New York, the creative group I was in was responsible for the Yellow Pages account. The most glamorous and fun part of the account to work on was the now classic "Let Your Fingers Do The Walking" television commercials. But an equally important but far less glamorous portion of the account was the series of ads we did that appeared in business magazines to encourage businesses to advertise in the Yellow Pages.

Gathering background for these ads took a lot of work. The writers on the account rotated responsibilities and, when a writer's turn came to do a series of these ads, he would travel to a city where the local Yellow Pages sales representative would set up interviews with businesspeople who had enjoyed success from their Yellow Pages ads. Each ad we created from these interviews would run in trade publications focused on that particular business category.

After doing these interviews for a while I learned to listen for headlines. When a realtor told me that right after his ad appeared in the Yellow Pages his listings jumped 20%, a skyrocket would go off in my head. I knew instantly that I had a headline for my ad— "My business jumped 20% when my ad ran in the Yellow Pages."

Or when the owner of the mortuary told me that the number of funerals he held jumped 50 percent when his ad appeared, I was pleased...not because so many people had passed away but because I knew I had the makings of a good strong ad for the Yellow Pages.

The ads we created based on these interview missions weren't award winners but they were definitely client winners. When they appeared, sales of Yellow Pages ads by AT&T invariably increased and it made for a very happy client.

One day I learned through the grapevine that one of the writers in our group, I'll call him Chad, had gone on a job interview at another agency. That happens all the time in the agency business because generally the best way to get the biggest raises was to change agencies. As happy as I was at my current job, when I got a call from a recruiter about the same position Chad had gone for, I decided to go for an interview.

Armed with my portfolio, I visited the agency and talked to the person who was looking for a writer. As he reviewed my ads, he muttered something that sounded like "I've seen these somewhere." I had no idea what he was talking about and after about 15 minutes he thanked me and said he'd keep me in mind for the position.

Then, on my way back to the agency it suddenly hit me: Chad had shown the interviewer some of my ads passing them off as his. I was stunned. Our creative group was like a family and besides working hard, we spent more than a few hours in Madison Avenue bars drinking together and laughing. I couldn't get my head around the idea that Chad would take credit for doing some of my ads.

But what amazed me more than anything was that I stayed silent. I said nothing to Chad about his intellectual theft and even to this day I'm not really sure why I did nothing. A few days later, Chad announced that he was leaving for another position. It was the job I had interviewed for. I was angrier with myself for my silence than with him. I didn't go to his farewell party.

Happily though, I still liked my agency and the people I worked with. So I continued to smile although secretly smarting from the evil deed Chad had done.

But apparently there is justice in the world, even in the world of advertising. About a month later, I was in my boss' office when he got a phone call from Chad. He hated his new job. His new agency was not known as a creative place so he was having difficulty selling any good ideas he had. He didn't like his boss very much and his client was very difficult to deal with.

To make this phone call, Chad had swallowed his pride and asked my boss if he could have his job back. But he couldn't. Soon after he had left, they had hired a new writer to replace him. I had liked the new writer from the beginning because he was both fun and friendly. Now I liked him even more because his being there had prevented Chad from coming back.

Sometimes crime really does not pay.

* * *

In the fifties and sixties, one of my favorite comedians was Professor Irwin Corey. Little did I know that in several years he was going to have a profound effect on my life.

Appearing on television in his formal swallowtail coat, sloppy string tie, mussed hair and thick who-knows-where-it-came-from accent, he delivered unique offbeat humor. I, along with millions of television viewers, found him hysterical.

That's why, whenever he appeared at a nightclub in New York's Greenwich Village, my friends and I would never miss a chance to see him. When we sat down at a table before his act, we always expected the unexpected. And he never failed to deliver. Then one night he said something that was life-changing for me.

During one routine he announced, "Remember, friends. Don't put off until tomorrow what you can do today. (Pause) Because if you like it today, you can do it again tomorrow."

We all laughed uproariously but for the rest of the evening I couldn't get that thought out of my head. It was funny to me but profound. The next day I asked an art director in my agency to make that into a small sign which I hung on the wall of my office. It hung there for years and when I changed agencies it followed me to my new office.

By this time I had married an actress who one day called me in the office.

"I just got an offer to do film work…in Madrid."

I asked her how long the job would be.

"At least two months, maybe more. We have to go."

It was incredibly tempting. Living in Spain all that time and maybe traveling around Europe afterwards. But I couldn't just quit my job and take that much time off. My career was going well and I was afraid a hiatus like that would be damaging.

"We just can't do it," I reluctantly told her.

We hung up and I sat there dejected. It sounded like a great opportunity for her career but…I'd love to take the time off but… There were buts in every direction I looked. Leaving my job and going away for that long, no matter how exciting, just wouldn't work.

Then my eyes fell on the sign that had hung on my wall for years. "Don't put off until tomorrow what you can do today. Because if you like it today you can do it again tomorrow."

It struck me like a lightning bolt. I just couldn't pass up this once-in-a-lifetime opportunity to live in Spain for months. I called my wife and told her "We're going. I'll explain later." With that, I got up and walked into the creative director's office and announced to him that I was reluctantly resigning. I explained why and told him how difficult a decision it was but that I knew it was the right one.

About 10 minutes later he walked into my office. "I've spoken to the executive committee and we're not accepting your resignation. We're giving you a leave of absence instead."

I was stunned. He assured me that I could take off as long as I liked and could come back with my job waiting for me. I could never have dreamed of such a great response. I thanked him and left for home to tell my wife the good news.

When we were in Madrid, my wife worked in commercials intermittently for three months. In between her jobs we traveled throughout Spain in our little Renault visiting lovely landmarks like Valencia, Seville and Granada. We even took the ferry across the straits of Gibraltar for a brief visit to Morocco.

While we were in Madrid, I got a surprise: work. My agency, Needham Harper & Steers, had a European affiliate with an office in Madrid. In hopes of finding an excuse to write off at least a portion of the trip as a business expense, I called the creative director. When he answered, I introduced myself. He responded immediately in a wonderfully rich British accent, "Don, where the hell have you been? I've been waiting for your call."

I was stunned. He explained that my boss in New York, knowing that I was going to Madrid, had written a letter commending me to him. He had a project that he wanted me to work on. And so it was that with my freshman Spanish, I helped them with a business pitch for a prospective account. And I earned enough pesetas (those were the pre-Euro days) to pay for a goodly number of tapas (Spanish hors d'oeuvres) and tintos (glasses of red wine) during our stay in Madrid.

Once my wife's work was finished, we climbed in our car and traveled through France, Italy, Greece and England for another seven months. The most popular travel book in those days was *Europe on $10 a Day* and we proved that you could really do it.

And when we got back to New York, my job was waiting for me, as promised, along with a carton containing almost a year's worth of my mail.

Some 12 years later my life had changed dramatically. My wife and I had divorced and I had moved to Los Angeles. At the Los Angeles office of Foote Cone Belding, one of the accounts I was responsible for was AM/PM Minimarkets, convenience stores that were part of the ARCO gasoline corporation.

At one point, ARCO was holding a national conference in Las Vegas for AM/PM franchisees and the festivities would include a musical. My job was to write the lyrics for the songs in the show. Being a musician myself, I enjoyed the challenge.

When the conference convened at the MGM Grand Hotel, I flew to Las Vegas to see my work come alive onstage. The night of the performance, I sat up in the director's booth with the show's producer as the house lights dimmed. I knew nothing about the show other than my songs and I was surprised and pleased to see the master of ceremonies who stepped out on the stage to tumultuous applause.

Professor Irwin Corey, without knowing it,
helped me make a major decision in my life

It was Professor Irwin Corey. He still wore the same swallow-tail coat, string tie and shaggy haircut and his humor was just as original and funny as I had remembered from so many years ago. The musical with Corey ad-libbing in between numbers was a hit and as the final curtain rang down, the audience rose and applauded wildly.

I immediately leapt out of the booth and ran down the stairs towards the stage. When the applause died down and the house lights came up, I climbed the stage and went through the curtain. And there was Irwin Corey standing there. I went up to him and introduced myself. He was very affable and still the same character he was onstage. Then I told him the story of his miraculous "Don't put off until tomorrow" line that helped me make a major decision in my life and I thanked him for it.

He smiled a big smile, shook my hand and said, "You know what that means, Don? That means you have to buy me a drink."

And so it was that we retired to the bar, had a couple of drinks and parted friends. The drinks I bought him weren't nearly enough payback for what he had done for me. But that I could thank him at all was wonderful.

∞ **9** ∞

ALCOHOL ON THE AVENUE

If you were to believe the early episodes of *Mad Men*, in the sixties Madison Avenue folks swam in a sea of alcohol. In the show, when someone entered an executive's office, they were invariably greeted with an empty glass and a decanter of whiskey, even in morning meetings.

I don't know if it was like that before I entered the business but by the time I did, the days of the fabled three-martini lunch were fading. And that was just as well because, frankly, I wasn't very good at handling my liquor. Even one glass of wine at lunch made me sleepy and, besides being unable to write much, I didn't relish the idea of someone coming into my office at three in the afternoon to see me snoozing at my desk. But I did occasionally make an exception. And once when I did, I learned a valuable lesson.

I went to lunch in a Madison Avenue restaurant with an agency producer I did a lot of work with. I don't remember what the occasion was but Ed suggested we have a drink and I agreed. I ordered a Bloody Mary while Ed ordered a scotch and soda. I was surprised.

"Ed," I exclaimed. "When we get back to the office they'll smell that booze on your breath. That's why I'm having a vodka drink."

"Yes," Ed said, "but you know that we're not going to stop at just one drink. And when we get back to the office, at least they'll know I'm drunk. They'll just think you're stupid."

I thought about his wisdom for a moment and called the waiter over. "Make that a scotch and soda."

And from that day on when I did have a drink at lunch I made sure it wasn't vodka. I'd rather be thought of as drunk, not stupid.

Ed followed his own advice to me well. Perhaps too well. A few months later at our agency Christmas party, true to his advice, he drank Scotch so that people knew he was drunk. However he drank so much of it that at one point he climbed on a desk, unzipped his fly and, to his everyone's amusement, peed on the carpet.

It amused everyone except the head of the office who made Ed pay for the heavy-duty carpet cleaning, proving that what Ed had advised me months before—that he'd rather be thought of as drunk, not stupid—was only partially true. You could also be both drunk *and* stupid.

* * *

In the years that followed, when it came to drinking I was something of a lightweight, drinking mixed drinks like Brandy Alexanders and Black Russians rather than the macho Scotch-and-sodas that were more of an advertising industry standard. But I didn't realize how much of a lightweight image I was projecting until one evening when a group of us were out of town. We had just won the Xerox account and were spending a week with them in Rochester getting to know the people and learning more about their business.

After a full day of meetings, six of us went to a local restaurant to have a drink and dinner. When the waiter was taking our drink orders and got to me, he asked me what I'd like. Before I could answer, one of my senior account executives answered for me.

"Give that young fellow anything with foam on the top."

Until that moment, I had no idea of how much of a lightweight I was…alcohol-wise.

Several years later when I was leaving the agency to depart for Los Angeles, they gave me a farewell lunch at a local restaurant. The group called on me to say a few words and in the course of my reminiscing I told the foam-on-top story.

It got quite a few laughs but also got something more than that. Unbeknownst to me, while I talked, my boss, Barry Biederman, ordered a round of drinks with foam on the top for the whole room. As I was about to step down, I heard the clink of some two dozen foam-topped glasses clinking in their farewell toast to me.

* * *

During my third year as a copywriter, I got my first taste of expense account living and I found it could be a headache. Literally.

One of the accounts I worked on was Ballantine's Scotch, a fine whisky imported by our client, 21 Brands. Our group had been charged with developing a new ad campaign for the product and had come up with an approach that we liked very much: "How good is Ballantine's Scotch? Ask any bartender."

We assumed that even though few people would actually ask their bartender, there was a tone of confidence in the line that spoke well of the brand. And if people did ask, they would probably get a positive answer because not only was Ballantine's considered a good scotch, it also commanded a premium price at the bar.

Although I hadn't come up with the line, I did come up with a way to help sell it to the client. Why not actually go around asking bartenders how good they thought Ballantine's was and record their answers? We could edit together any positive comments we got and, although we couldn't offer it as good, objective research, it would be a colorful way to present the campaign and would give the clients a level of confidence in the line.

In order to not influence the bartenders' answers, I wanted to record them without their knowledge. So I looked in the Yellow

Pages and found a store that apparently rented equipment to spies. It was filled with surveillance equipment—microphones that could hear conversations at great distances, telephone bugging devices and the like. I was fascinated. I told the clerk what I wanted to do and he pulled what I needed right from under the counter. It was a perfectly innocent-looking attaché case. But inside was a tape recorder sitting in a cushioning nest of soft foam. To record, I just had to lift up the right latch and the sensitive microphone hidden under the handle captured every word. James Bond meets Madison Avenue.

I called my wife, told her about my secret mission and invited her to join me. So, on the stroke of five, we walked into the first bar, a watering hole on Madison Avenue popular with people in the ad business. I sat down, placed the attaché case on the bar and lifted the right latch. I had planned my approach carefully, just like Mr. Bond would. I couldn't just blurt out the question. It had to sound natural. I ordered a scotch and soda and, as the bartender reached to pour the usual well scotch, I interrupted him.

"Say, how good is that Ballantine's Scotch?," I inquired in a casual method-acting style.

"Pretty good stuff," he replied. It worked! I was thrilled but kept my Bond-esque cool. "Would you like Ballantine's?," he asked. "No, just being curious. Make it a Dewar's." I already knew what Ballantine's tasted like and had decided that this expense account mission was an opportunity to taste the competition.

There was no shortage of bars on Manhattan's East Side and we rarely had to walk more than a minute between them. By the fourth or fifth one, I had come to a profound realization. Contrary to what my mother had taught me at home, it wasn't necessary to drink to the last drop at every stop. In fact, I had better not. With some quick math, which was getting more and more difficult as my research project continued, I realized that if I drank just half a drink at each, I could double the number of bars I could visit.

My wife wisely declined to continue the research and went home. As the evening progressed, I decided I really liked doing advertising research. In fact, by then I liked just about everybody and everything. The bartenders were cooperating—no really spectacular responses but most were positive enough to use in the presentation tape. Somewhere around the twelfth bar, I came to a reluctant realization: my efficiency was diminished.

It came over me gradually. As I was walking toward the twelfth or thirteenth bar, I realized that my attaché case/secret tape recorder was getting heavy and my tongue was getting thick. I had better terminate soon. Maybe just one more bartender.

I chose as my grand finale a chic East Side restaurant named *Sign of the Dove*, as well-known for its bright yellow exterior as for its food. In the bar, I ordered and before the bartender poured, asked about Ballantine's. He looked at me with a big smile on his face.

"Are you kidding," he answered. "I wouldn't drink any other scotch if you paid me." I had struck gold. The man was a walking commercial for the brand. He went into such paroxysms of praise for it that I was embarrassed to ask for any other brand and had my client's product as my nightcap. What a coup. I was ecstatic. What a capper to the mission. That was it.

With the help of the doorman, I made it to a taxi and home. I walked into the bedroom where my wife lay reading. "Hello," I said. "G'night," I added, and fell facedown, fully clothed, onto the bed.

Seven hours later, I awoke with a head the size of Brooklyn. As my wife gave me a huge cup of coffee, I remembered the *Sign of the Dove* bartender. I reached for the attaché case and backed up the tape to my last interview. "Wait till you hear this one."

I hit "Play." It was a woman speaking. The only female bartender I had talked to was at the next-to-the-last bar. The crushing truth struck me: I had been so drunk that I had forgotten to turn on the recorder for the greatest interview I had gotten.

As it turned out, it didn't matter. My boss told me after his presentation to the client that the client, a mercurial man given to quick and strong judgments, had hated the "Ask any bartender" campaign so immediately and violently that my boss didn't even bother to play my bartender tape. It would not only have been futile...it probably would have angered the man even more.

But the mission was not a total loss. I learned I was able to use an expense account with the best of them. Although I was able to sample upwards of a dozen brands of scotch that night, it took me about five years before I was able to drink scotch again.

* * *

Knowing you won't have to drive after a heavy drinking session is a big encouragement for consuming alcohol. But an even bigger one is knowing you won't have to pay for it. The expense account is probably responsible for more hangovers than anything else in the modern world.

In the chic restaurants and fine hotels we often patronized, the expense accounts we turned in were often grotesque. But if we could justify them in some way, they were usually approved. But on one occasion my expense account tested the limits...and it wasn't even my doing.

We were in Acapulco shooting a commercial for our Western Airlines account. After we had finished a tough two-day shoot featuring the famous Acapulco cliff divers, I threw a wrap party for cast, crew and agency people in my room at the Las Brisas hotel.

Knowing the cost of alcohol in the hotel, I had gone into town and brought in plenty of liquor and wine. But one of the agency account executives apparently found my selection inadequate and, unbeknownst to me, went to my room bar and decided to sample its vast array of liquors. He opened seven different bottles and took a sip from each. Even though I didn't see him at the time, I was positive that he opened exactly seven bottles because the next day my room bill featured charges for the purchase of seven bottles…a total of $245.

My expense-account-approving grace was the fact that two of our clients had been at my party so I could write the evening off as client entertainment.

* * *

One of the things I enjoyed most about advertising was the diversity of products and services I got to work on. In the course of a week I might work on a TV commercial for a European sports car, a radio spot for a children's aspirin, a newspaper ad for scotch whiskey and a magazine ad for canned ham. It was stimulating to have to switch mental channels to address each creative challenge. And when a unique product came along that I had never worked on before, it was even more refreshing.

Not surprisingly, as a kid from Brooklyn, I hadn't come into much contact with many tractors. And, as it turned out, in the process of working on this new category, I would have a chance to create a new sport.

The Homelite Company was known for their chainsaws and when my creative director called me and my creative partner, Peter Tiisler, into his office and told us he was assigning the Homelite account to us, we weren't overjoyed. Chainsaws weren't the most exciting products.

But, he explained, we wouldn't be marketing their chainsaws. Homelite was launching a line of lawn and garden tractors, miniature versions of the farmer's friend. I liked the idea that it would be our job to introduce them to amateur gardeners across the country. But Peter, as an art director, was really turned on by his task of designing the all-important paint scheme for the tractors. If the little tractors were attractive, they would draw buyers who would proudly ride them back and forth across their lawns cutting the grass and, just as important, showing them off to their envious neighbors.

We set to work creating print ads and a television commercial to introduce the tractors to home gardeners. And Peter began designing a paint scheme for them that would draw attention—and buyers.

After several weeks, we presented our work to the client who was very pleased. They had scheduled a grand opening to introduce the tractors to their sales team at their factory in South Carolina. The look of the tractors was a closely guarded secret and their unveiling at that opening would be a big moment. If the sales people were excited by the products, their job of selling them would be easier and would undoubtedly be more successful.

There was no time to set up the assembly line to paint the tractors so the only way to prepare them for the meeting was to hand-paint several. And who better to paint them than the person who designed the paint scheme: Peter. And who better to assist him than his tractor teammate: me. I had absolutely zero painting skills but I was a good cheerleader for Peter who needed all the cheerleading he could get.

We flew down to South Carolina the afternoon before the unveiling. The grand opening was scheduled for 8 o'clock in the morning but we couldn't get into the factory to begin painting until it closed at 9 o'clock that night. So we had time for a leisurely dinner accompanied by a couple of drinks. As we finished, we decided that just a couple of drinks wouldn't get us through the long night ahead. So before grabbing a cab to the factory, we stopped at a nearby liquor store and stocked up with some vodka along with some health-giving orange juice.

The night watchman let us in and showed us to the assembly line where the new equipment sat along with the paints, brushes and masking tape we'd be using. The factory was deathly still and dark other than the bright spotlights that shown down on the factory floor where we'd be working. After a toast to our mission, Peter set out to work. Other than handing Peter a brush or tape when he needed it, I was useless. I had been defacing coloring books ever since pre-school, never able to color an object without going over a line. To do that with these prototypes with our tight schedule would be disastrous. My job was to keep the atmosphere light and our glasses filled as Peter painstakingly painted the design on each piece of equipment. The work was demanding. The hours rolled by slowly and the vodka gradually disappeared.

Then, in the early hours of the morning, with the vodka gone, I sat on one of the unpainted tractors and discovered it had a key in its ignition. I turned the key and the engine roared into life. I shifted it into gear, twisted the throttle and the tractor lurched off the assembly line and zoomed across the floor. What a rush! I careened around trash barrels, bins of equipment parts and half-built tractors.

When Peter saw the fun I was having, he climbed on another tractor and turned the key. In seconds he was chasing me around the factory floor. The combination of fatigue and vodka worked their magic on us and we whooped and hollered as we tore through the empty factory.

As he passed an open janitor's closet, Peter stopped, reached inside and pulled out two brooms. I braked alongside him and he tossed one of the brooms to me. And at that moment, a new sport was born—Small Tractor Jousting. Peter drove to the opposite side of the open area we were in, steered to face me and mounted his broom under his arm, bristles pointed forward. I did the same and when he shouted "Go!" we drove toward each other at full speed…which on a small lawn and garden tractor wasn't very fast at all.

Fortunately, we were so drunk our broom/lances each missed. But our jousting continued. We turned our valiant metal steeds for a second pass and charged again. This time, Peter's broom connected and got me in the shoulder. And it hurt. I let out a cry of pain and dropped my broom. I wasn't really hurt but, liquor notwithstanding, we realized at that moment that what we were doing could be dangerous. We dismounted and looked at our watches. We really ought to take a brief nap. The paint on the equipment needed to dry more before we moved it outside to the show area on the lawn just outside the assembly line.

We lay down on the floor and went out instantly.

We would have slept most of the next day if the night watchman hadn't shaken Peter at 7:40 a.m. We had only twenty minutes to set up the equipment display for the show. With feet dragging and heads aching we moved the freshly painted tractors outside and placed them behind the curtain that had been set up on the lawn.

Just as we were finishing, the president of Homelite came in, looked at his tractors, now decorated in their bright new colors, and smiled. He liked what he saw.

When the sales staff had gathered on the lawn, the president gave a brief upbeat introduction to the new products and then, with a flourish, the curtains parted and there, in their newly-painted glory, was Homelite's brand new line of products. The reception was great and the sales staff applauded enthusiastically. But it wasn't music to Peter and my ears. Our heads hurt too much to enjoy it.

We had double satisfaction—we had not only done a good job for our client but in the process had created a new sport—Small Tractor Jousting.

Happily, the tractors went on to sell well. Unhappily, the jousting never caught on.

* * *

Most of the alcohol-related stories I remember from the advertising business were humorous. But, as in real life, several were far from funny. One of them involved a very nice woman I worked with.

An agency's media department makes recommendations to clients on how their advertising dollars should be spent. What media would be the most effective for the client? Television? Radio? Newspapers? Magazines? Internet? Direct mail? A combination of these? Because of the agency media staff's purchasing powers, the people who sell time for television and radio commercials and space for print and Internet ads work hard cultivating relationships. Forging good relations with agency media people is key to their jobs and success and so they lavish a lot of attention on them. For one person I worked with, this attention had tragic results.

The media representatives I met were generally intelligent and attractive and, as Willie Loman described himself in *Death of a Salesman*, had a shine on their shoes and a smile on their faces. Armed with their charm along with healthy expense accounts, they spent much time and money entertaining people in agency media departments.

Ruth was a media buyer at one of my agencies. She was single and, from those of us who dealt with her, apparently lonely. As a key person on our $13,000,000 advertising account, media reps courted her constantly. Hardly a day went by when she wasn't taken out to lunch by a media rep, generally an attractive man.

I soon learned that it wasn't a good idea to have a meeting with her after 2 p.m. The good life she was living had become too good and she had become an alcoholic. By the afternoon, her speech and her thinking were slurred by one too many Jack Daniels. And the party often continued after work when she was entertained at dinner by another media rep, eager to dig into her client's wallet.

But unhappily, it finally caught up with Ruth. The agency media director, a very kind and caring man, had protected her for too long. But he realized that, with the combination of her alcoholic reputation in the industry and the continual drop in her productivity, she had become a liability to the agency. Reluctantly he knew he had to let her go.

She moved north from Los Angeles to Santa Barbara and

briefly worked at a small agency there. But it was too close to L.A. and the ad community knew about her. She couldn't make it there. So she moved back to her native Texas.

But even that wasn't far enough away from L.A. Her reputation pursued her all the way to the Rio Grande. She tried for months but couldn't find a job there. For many years she had believed that people had wined and dined her because of her charm and wit. She hadn't accepted the fact that it was her purchasing power that was the magnet that drew people to her. She had confused friendship with business-ship.

Unemployed and now drinking uncontrollably, she couldn't face it anymore. One evening she checked into a motel. The next morning the maid found her lifeless body.

At her old agency, when we heard the news we were all very saddened. But at least we knew that her longstanding and terrible pain was finally over.

* * *

Besides the weather, the palm trees, the lovely girls and the lifestyle, there was something else that drew me to California—a beverage. During my first stay in the Beverly Hills hotel, we went to the Polo Lounge and I ordered a drink that sounded good—a Ramos Fizz.

I was already famous (or infamous) at my agency for my love of foamy, fizzy drinks and the description on the menu filled the bill. Made with gin, egg whites, heavy cream, sugar and orange flower water, all whipped into a frothy foam, it was my kind of drink. I loved it and, calories notwithstanding, enjoyed it throughout my stay.

But on my return to New York, when I asked bartenders for a Ramos Fizz, they looked at me blankly. Apparently, the New Orleans drink had made it west to Los Angeles but not north to New York. And thus my lust for L.A. was enhanced by the availability of this magic potion.

One day in the early '70's, Judy Wald, the major recruiter for creative people in New York, called and asked me if I'd be willing to move to the Los Angeles office of BBDO advertising. With visions of sand, sea, palm trees and Ramos Fizzes dancing in my head I instantly said "Absolutely."

And my love of Ramos Fizzes never left me. They figured in an enjoyable event I hosted at the agency. We had won a new account and I had the best way to celebrate—a Ramos Fizz party in the creative department's art studio. It's not an easy drink to fix but, as VP/Creative Director/Bartender, I was able to keep two Waring Blenders going for hours turning out gallons of the Fizzes for a very, very happy staff.

The party and the drink were hits and I received the ultimate compliment from one of my copywriters. He liked my Fizzes so much that he got a bit tipsy and we wouldn't let him drive home. He slept it off on a couch in his office. What made me consider that such a compliment was that, according to his religion's convictions, he shouldn't have been drinking at all.

∞ 10 ∞

ADVERTISING AND MUSIC — SCORES THAT SELL

Television commercials often contain a not-so-secret weapon that can make them incredibly more effective—music. A good commercial, along with its message, conveys an emotion—humor, fear, patriotism or any one of a dozen emotions. Whatever the emotion is, music reaches a primal area of our brain and enhances that emotion. Think of the feeling you get watching a movie of the American flag waving silently. Then add *God Bless America* to the soundtrack and see how much deeper that feeling goes.

The right music can make a commercial more memorable and, hopefully, more effective.

Thanks to that primal area, some of my favorite moments in my career have been in dimly lit recording studios. I've loved music ever since, as a little kid, I sat on the floor playing with toys and listening to my mom play *Parade of the Wooden Soldiers* on the piano. I had started taking piano lessons at nine and had become a fairly proficient purveyor of popular music. So when I wrote a commercial that called for musical scoring, I was in heaven knowing that I'd soon be sitting in a recording studio watching masterful musicians helping to make my commercial come alive.

When we hired a composer to write the music, I'd be in the initial meeting with him to discuss the commercial and, in general, the kind of music that might work best. Should it be warm and friendly to make the product likeable? Or humorous to strengthen the smiles the visuals hopefully will create? Or should it create tension with a big dramatic flourish at the climax when the product turns out to be a hero? The possibilities are endless.

Once the composer had a general direction, he went off on his own to turn the abstract ideas we agreed on into music. He would return days later to play a demo of what he's written and, if we liked it, we were off to my favorite location—the recording studio.

* * *

The studio musicians who record music for commercials are often some of the best musicians in the business. Many times, as I looked from the engineer's booth into the studio, I saw musicians I had seen on top TV shows or at major jazz clubs. They have to be good because often the music they're called on to play isn't easy. And when you're paying two dozen musicians in a studio and the clock is ticking, a player who can't get his or her part right can make it an expensive session.

Sitting in the booth with a recording engineer and the agency producer with the sheet music in front of me, I was always amazed at how the musicians could play often complex and difficult passages the first time around. As union musicians, they were paid well but they were worth every penny.

At one point I enjoyed a very nice bonus for hiring a top composer.

When I first moved out to Los Angeles from New York I had to learn about the talent pool that I would be able to choose from— the commercial directors, the photographers and the illustrators— to bring our ads and commercials to life. I spent hours viewing the reels of the directors and the portfolios of the photographers and illustrators. But my favorite part of that research was sitting for hours listening to the music of the composers in the Los Angeles area. With the film industry based there, there were a lot of talented people I would be able to choose from.

I found my first composer unexpectedly. While I was watching a commercial for Santa Anita racetrack, I realized that the music had given me goose bumps. The composer's name was Don Piestrup.

I called him and found him very personable and soon hired him to score a commercial we had written. He did a good job, was easy to work with and the recording session was very enjoyable. It led to a series of jobs and sessions with Don that I always looked forward to. It was in one of these sessions that I had one of my favorite moments of my career.

Don had composed a score that called for some twenty musicians, a larger-than-usual commercial complement. As he stood with a baton in the studio, I sat along with my agency producer and the recording engineer in the glass booth with the music score before me. With my past musical training, a great part of my enjoyment in recording sessions was watching as the musical notes on the score came to life before my very ears.

Don spoke to the musicians and then raised his baton for a rehearsal. On his downbeat, they started playing and, as they did, I followed the score with an admiring smile on my face. Parts of the music were complex but they played on perfectly.

As I listened, I had an idea and as soon as the music ended I hit the button on the microphone that spoke through the studio loudspeakers.

"Don," I asked, "would it sound a little richer if, in bar 32, instead of an F major you played an F major seventh?" I was suggesting that he add an E-note to the chord.

Every musician's eyes turned to the glass booth where I was sitting. Ad agency people didn't generally have a good reputation among the performers, directors and others who executed their ideas. Because they were the ones who did the hiring, agency people often used their positions to offer gratuitous ideas in areas they were completely uninformed about. Their ideas could be impractical, expensive, undoable and sometimes even dumb.

So when an agency guy like me suggested a change in the score, there was a sea of rolling eyes in the studio. But Don, with a smile on his face, turned back to the orchestra.

"The agency guy says to add an E-note in bar 32 so let's try it."

On his downbeat they played the piece again and at bar 32 played my F major seventh chord. The next moment his baton signaled "Cut" to the orchestra. Spontaneously, as a single person, they turned to me in the glass booth smiling and began applauding, their hands coming together and the string players tapping their bows on their music stands.

Don smiled. "Well what do you know? The guy from the agency got it right. Well done, Don."

And that's how, by adding one note to a chord, I got one of the major thrills of my advertising career.

* * *

I enjoyed working with Don from the very first recording session I did with him. But it was something more than his music and his good sense of humor that brought me and my agency compatriots back to him repeatedly: wine. He had a very large and wonderful collection that he generously brought out during our often long and late recording sessions at Bell Sound Studios in Hollywood. Even the score for a brief 30-second commercial could take hours to record and edit and Don's wine made that time go by much more quickly.

And the quality of Don's wine was superb because it had to be. He was in a silent wine competition with another fine composer, John Tartaglia. Don and John vied for the finest wine collection and we clients benefited from the contest. There were no prizes other than bragging rights but that was enough for these two good friends to bring their best to the studio. And we were the beneficiaries.

The result was that no recording session was ever too long or too late. We always enjoyed every musical bar we heard and every wine-filled sip we took.

* * *

Being in advertising gave me an opportunity to thank someone who did me a favor he never knew he had done. When I attended Hamilton College in upstate New York, it had a well-deserved reputation for being a party school. At the time, Hamilton was an all-male school so, to break up the masculine monotony, we had lots of parties…good, well-lubricated ones. The best were our semi-raucous parties that went over entire weekends like our Spring Houseparty, Fall Houseparty and Winter Carnival.

Hamilton's reputation for having good parties was well-known and getting dates for them wasn't too difficult, even with complete strangers. In the organization I belonged to, Squires Club, if we had a party weekend coming up, one of us would get on the phone and call one of the girl's dormitories at Syracuse University and say we needed six girls for the weekend. No problem. On Friday evening, at Utica's Union Station, when the train arrived from Syracuse, standing on the platform were six girls eager to join in the Hamilton festivities.

At Squires, there was a protocol we followed for pairing off. The guy who made the call went to the station and had first pick of the girls. Any Squires officer had next pick. Then the other guys who drove to the station chose. After that it was each man for himself.

From the time our dates arrived on Friday evening until we waved goodbye to them on Sunday evening, the hours were filled with lots of laughing, liquor and, if things went well, loving.

One of my favorite weekends was Jazz Party. There was lots of good music at events through the two days but the heart of the weekend was on Saturday night when the college always hired a great band to entertain us.

On Jazz Party weekend in my junior year I had gotten one of the anonymous dates from Syracuse I had met at the Utica train station. She was cute and friendly and as I drove back to the campus we looked forward to a fun weekend.

The musical highlight of the weekend was a concert by Don Elliott, a masterful jazz musician I had always admired. His unique style was to play two instruments at the same time. While he blew a haunting melody on the mellophone, a cousin to the ethereal French horn, he accompanied himself on the equally mellow vibes, one of my favorite instruments.

Don had the crowd in the palm of his hands from the very first number. My date and I sat near the bandstand holding hands casually as Elliott went from an upbeat high-energy number to a slow languid piece. But to me the absolute highlight of the evening was his rendition of the classic standard, *Laura.* The song had always been a favorite of mine but I had never heard it rendered as gently and romantically. As the notes floated out to us from his horn and vibes and echoed off the high ceiling, my date's hold on my hand tightened and we moved closer together. The number set the tone for a very romantic evening, one for which I would be always grateful to Don.

Eleven years passed and by then I was well into my advertising career. I had written a commercial that called for a musical score but I wasn't senior enough in the agency to choose a composer. So the choice was up to my agency producer. I was surprised and excited when my producer came to my office and announced that he had hired Don Elliott to score my commercial.

The next day we went to Don's office where, partnered with the legendary Quincy Jones, Don worked. We discussed the commercial and what we thought the best musical approach to this score would be. Then I did something I never thought I'd have a chance to do: I thanked him. I reminded him of his gig at Hamilton College the decade before and, more importantly, his incredible rendition of *Laura* that had led to my very romantic evening.

Don was all smiles and thanked me for thanking him. He had won musical awards he was proud of but there was something special about this compliment that he said he was especially pleased with. The big grin on his face proved that he meant it.

* * *

The music in the movie *Black Orpheus* instantly made it one of my favorite movies of all time.

The movie was a modern retelling of the Greek legend in which Orpheus travels to the Underworld to try to bring his dead wife Eurydice back to earth. Hades, god of the Underworld, agrees to allow Orpheus to bring her back on one condition: that Orpheus never looks back until they are both on the earth. At the last minute, something causes Orpheus to look back and they are both doomed to the Underworld forever.

Black Orpheus transported the legend to Brazil during the festival of Carnival. The costumes, the parades, the drama were all unique and colorful but it was the music that was spellbinding. The haunting theme that appeared all throughout the film was *Manha do Carnaval—Carnival Morning—*a haunting bossa nova written by Brazilian guitarist Luiz Bonfa. I saw the movie three times and was enthralled, hypnotized mostly by the music.

In the mid-60s I was an active member of the New York branch of the Emmy-sponsoring Academy of Television Arts and Sciences and I had volunteered to help develop special events for Academy members to enjoy. When I was helping plan one of these events I got a phone call from an officer of the Academy. He had gotten a call from an agent who represented Luiz Bonfa. Bonfa had come to the United States recently and was eager to make his presence known. His agent believed that appearing before members of the Television Academy would be a good way to spread the word.

I hung up the phone very excited even though I had no idea

how we would integrate Bonfa into the event we were planning. It had nothing to do with music, movies or guitars. My task was to find some way to make his appearance relevant to the event.

I was sure of one thing—before he could appear in my event I would have to meet him. Eager to help launch him in America, his people readily agreed to set up a meeting in his apartment on the Upper Westside of Manhattan. I was both excited and nervous. My career was relatively new and I had not as yet dealt with famous talent like Bonfa.

But I needn't have been concerned. Bonfa answered the door himself despite the fact that at least half a dozen of his associates were in the room. He smiled winningly and shook my hand vigorously. I liked him already.

My purpose in the meeting was to get to know him and his music. I believed that would help me find a way to integrate him into the Academy event. When I looked around the room, I knew I was in the right place. Leaning against the wall were eight guitars. Bonfa and I spent a few minutes chatting and getting to know each other and then I asked him a question about his music. It was about his creation of *Manha do Carnaval*, the haunting theme of the movie. He thought about his answer for a moment and then did something unexpected.

Instead of answering it verbally, he walked over to the guitar wall and chose one of the eight guitars. Then, placing his foot on a small footrest, he played a piece of the theme to illustrate his brief answer.

I asked another question. To my surprise, he got up and selected a different guitar, responding with another portion of his music. For the next twenty minutes or so he spoke of the creative process he went through and why he chose to write it in a minor key. As he talked, he illustrated each point by playing chords, first isolating them then playing them in the haunting rhythm of the bossa nova. What fascinated me most was that he changed guitars frequently. Despite the fact that I played the piano and prided myself on having a pretty good musical ear, there was no way I could tell the subtle differences between guitars. But he obviously could.

I was enthralled. Delaying my departure as long as I could, I finally said goodnight to Bonfa and headed home to my apartment. I was really stoked and on the way I thought of a reasonable way to integrate him into our Academy program. In introducing him, the master of ceremonies could talk about the power of music to generate emotion in the television programs that members of the TV Academy were involved in. And one of the finest examples of emotion-generating music was the score of *Black Orpheus*. From that point on, the link to Bonfa was made and his introduction would be smooth and natural.

The night of the Academy event, Bonfa was introduced by our emcee and, before he played a note, got a standing ovation for his magnificent work in *Black Orpheus*. But that was just the beginning. Originally slated to play for fifteen minutes, he was an instant hit and, with the audience's encouragement, played for some 45 minutes. And he didn't need those eight guitars. One guitar was all he needed to capture and enthrall his audience.

For a long time after that I tried to write a commercial that justified hiring him to write the score. But his work was too exotic for the very unromantic accounts I worked on like Folger's Coffee, AMF Bowling and the Yellow Pages so I never got a chance to work with him. I had to be content with the masterful music he played for me on that memorable Night of the Eight Guitars.

∞ 11 ∞

A FEW LAST MAD MEN-TIONS

In the diverse and perverse universe of advertising I worked and lived in, I had adventures that I believe deserve telling but that don't fit neatly into the chapter subjects I've chosen.

But rather than losing them forever just because they don't fit neatly into a particular category, I've included them here. My logic for including them may be a bit sloppy, but to me neatness doesn't count if not using them means losing them.

Herewith, some random Mad Man memories:

My boss at Cunningham & Walsh in New York was Don Ayers, a fine writer as well as a delightful guy to work for. There was frequent laughter in his office, even during the high-stress, short deadline ad assignments that often came down. Don was usually the heart of the humor but in one memorable historic moment I was the source.

It was November 1965 and my wife and I were planning a trip to upstate New York that would require my taking an extra vacation day. For that I'd need Don's approval.

It was after five in the evening and several members of our creative group had gathered in Don's office for the usual post-workday glass of wine. I walked into his office and Don pointed to the wine bottle, silently offering me a glass of an inexpensive pinot noir. As I poured it, I spoke to him.

"Don, would it be okay if I extended my vacation by a day?"

Before he could answer, the lights in the office went out. I looked around and it appeared as if all the lights in the agency were dark. I ran to the window and looked out on Madison Avenue. It was completely black—street lights, traffic lights, interior lights in all the buildings. We didn't know it then but the Great Blackout of 1965 had begun and some 30 million people in the northeastern U.S. were suddenly without electricity.

Without skipping a beat, I turned to my boss.

"Don, you could have just said 'No'."

When Don stopped laughing he told me to take the extra day off. He probably would have given me the okay anyway but I think my ad-lib helped him make his decision.

* * *

One Christmas, a caring gesture by an advertising executive led my parents and me to one of the most joyous holidays we ever had.

Two weeks before Christmas, the head of our BBDO/West office, Jack Bernardi, sent out a memo to the staff. Instead of holding our annual agency Christmas party, it said we would take that money and buy gifts for a few needy families. As much fun— and often out of hand—our Christmas parties had been in the past, everybody loved this idea.

To choose the families that would receive our presents, Jack's secretary contacted one of Los Angeles' social service agencies and got a list of families who were receiving assistance. Out of that list, three needy families were chosen at random.

In a drawing, I picked a card that had the name of one of the families. I would be one of the three lucky Santa Clauses who'd go out and give happiness to a family that could use more of it. This was already a special holiday for me because my mom and dad were visiting me from Florida. To have them join with me in this mission made it even more enjoyable.

The family I had chosen, I learned, consisted of a single mother and her young boy. She was receiving social services and was substantially below the poverty level.

I called her, introduced myself and told her what we would like to do for her and her son. We wanted to buy presents to go under her Christmas tree. She responded that they had never had a Christmas tree...they never could afford one.

"We'll make it a Merry Christmas even without the tree," I assured her.

I asked her what was on her wish list and she didn't respond with the pretty dresses or dainty shoes I had expected. She said she'd like laundry detergent, bleach, a new mop to replace her old worn-out one and several other similar items that I had taken for granted my whole life.

I asked her about her 10-year-old son. What would he like for Christmas? Her list of his needs was similar—socks, underwear, a T-shirt and, maybe if we could afford it, a new pair of jeans because, she said, his one pair was very old and worn.

"What about toys?" I asked. When she heard this I could feel her excitement.

"He loves airplanes," she explained. "He would love a toy airplane."

I immediately envisioned a nice metal battery-powered jet plane model. But even before the image of that plane formed in my mind she continued, "You know, those little tiny wooden airplanes that he can throw and they fly around a little."

I was stunned. She was saying that he would be excited if he got a fifty-cent balsa wood glider. The reality of that hit me so hard I had difficulty speaking. For the first time in my life I understood what poverty was. I thanked her and told her I would call her to set up a time when we could bring them some presents. I could hear the gratitude in her voice as she thanked me and said goodbye.

The next day my mom, dad and I went shopping. We got the mother the necessities she asked for but we didn't stop there. My mom picked out a lovely apron, a sweater and several other items the mother would never buy for herself...or expect.

But the highlight of our shopping expedition was when we went into a toy store and I bought that big metal jet airliner that I had started to envision when his mother said he liked airplanes. It was battery-powered and when you pushed it along the floor, its lights lit and its engines made low-pitched whining sounds.

Then the day came when my mom, dad and I were to play Santa Claus. We arrived at their apartment and went to the door with three bags full of presents. When she greeted us, the mother was lovely, smiling and already grateful. But it was her boy who was really excited. She told us that he couldn't wait for Christmas and invited us to stay while they unwrapped their presents.

And we never could have anticipated what we saw. The mother's face lit up with every item she pulled from the bags, no matter how mundane. The detergent, mop and other household items all brought smiles to her face. But her smiles turned to a glow when she saw the unexpected apron, sweater and jacket.

Then it was her son's turn. I had kept the jet plane hidden in its own package. As he uncovered the socks, the underwear, the pair of jeans and the other necessities, he was pleased. But then I added as if it was an afterthought, "Oh yeah. Your mom said you liked planes. So we also got you this." And I revealed his toy jetliner.

He was stunned. His eyes and mouth opened wide in surprise as he ran over and took it from me. He had never received a present like that in his life. As he sat down on the floor and started playing with it, I looked around. Both mothers, his and mine, had smiles on their faces and tears in their eyes. It was a magic moment I'll never forget.

The next morning in the office I recounted the adventure. Everybody was thrilled. Giving up our office party was nothing compared to the joy everybody got from this mission.

But the mother and her son weren't the only ones to be surprised this Christmas. At 11 o'clock two days before Christmas, office head Jack Bernardi got on the PA system and announced that there would be an all-hands meeting in the conference room. When we entered we were amazed. There on the table and all around the room was liquor, wines, vittles, cakes and cookies for everyone.

From the very beginning, Jack had never intended for us to do without a Christmas party. His story about our giving up our party was just a bluff. Jack had always planned for us to have our party and to do good works at the same time.

He had proved to us that we could have our cake, give it away, and eat it too.

* * *

I entered one phase of my career totally unexpectedly. While I was at Needham Harper & Steers in New York I got an assignment to write a radio commercial for a Bristol-Myers product, 4-Way Nasal Spray. I wrote the commercial and showed it to the creative director who liked it. We decided that rather than my going to the client with the script and reading it for him it would be more effective if I would record it in the small recording studio we had in the agency and add some sound effects. I could then take the recorded cassette to the client and play it for him.

A few days later, the account executive and I went to Bristol Myers with the cassette. After some introductory remarks by the account executive, I pressed the Play button on the cassette player and out came the commercial. Sixty seconds later the client sat before us with a pleased smile on his face.

"I like it," he said. "Let's produce it. What's the next step?"

"We'll have to cast an announcer for this," I replied.

"What do you mean?" he said. "I like this guy. Use him."

"He's not a professional announcer," I said. "He's me."

"I don't care," my client responded. "I like it. I want to use you."

He wouldn't be shaken. He was insistent on using me. The account executive explained that our agency was a signatory to AFTRA, the union that governed radio commercials and I wasn't a union member.

"Well then," said our client. "Join the union."

I was very flattered and a little embarrassed. We went back to the agency and fortunately our producer knew a way for me to do the commercial without violating our agency's agreement with the union.

From that point on, in my career I occasionally was hired on a freelance basis to record voice tracks for both radio and television commercials. I enjoyed the work almost as much as the checks I received for it.

* * *

Growing up in Brooklyn, one of my favorite things to do was to take the subway to Coney Island. And one trip there had a pretty large affect on my life. On a trip to Coney with my cousin Bill Barnett when I was about 12 years old we decided to go into a recording booth. Its operation was simple. In those pre-audio tape days, you stood in the booth, put in a quarter and a red light turned on indicating that the small record under the needle in the machine was recording you.

When the red light glowed, Bill and I started babbling the first things that came to our minds. As I recall, I said something about riding a roller coaster and at the end of one minute the light turned off. Mission accomplished. At that point the needle dropped down on the record and we heard a playback of the last minute. What I heard shocked me. I recognized Billy but I had no idea who the other guy was until it struck me like a hammer. The other voice was me. It was the first time I heard myself as others heard me.

But what shocked me even more was how I spoke. I had had no idea that I had a horrendous Brooklyn accent. It upset me and when I took the record home I played it for my mom and dad. I asked them if I always talked like that. My mom said gently, "Yes you do, Donny." And I asked them from then on to please help me change it. Both of them had moderate New York accents but nothing as contorted as mine.

For the next several years before college I paid attention and with my folks' help managed to reduce the outrageous accent for something more moderate and civilized. I was able to clean it up so much that when I entered advertising I was occasionally hired to do voiceovers for radio and television commercials.

But some two decades after my Coney Island nightmare, my Brooklyn past came back not to harm me but to help me. By then I had moved to Los Angeles and even though I held senior jobs in two major agencies I occasionally was hired to do voiceovers.

One day I was hired to do a 60-second radio spot for Taco Bell. I had created numerous TV and radio spots so the studio was a familiar scene for me—a soundproof booth with a microphone and headphones and the studio where the producer and representatives from the ad agency sat. The only difference was that in this case I was in the booth and the agency people were on the other side of the soundproof glass listening to me and judging me.

At the producer's cue I read the commercial once. He liked the reading and gave me some direction which I followed for Take Two. He then told me to stand by. As I sat in the booth, I could see the producer and the agency people having a lively discussion but couldn't hear a word of it through the soundproof glass.

After a minute or two the producer got on the microphone, pressed his microphone button, and through my headphone said something I will never forget.

"Don, do you think it's possible that you can do this with a slight Brooklyn accent?"

At that moment my three years of acting training kicked in. Screwing up my face and acting puzzled I said, "Gee, I don't know if I can. I've never done it before but I'll give it a try."

For the next reading I put myself back decades into that recording booth in Coney Island and recreated a mild version of how I sounded then.

Dey loved it and dat's wot went on de air.

* * *

In the '70's a virtually unknown means of communication, Citizens Band radio, suddenly leapt into popularity. And that leap led me to one of the wildest commercial shoots I ever was on.

At BBDO we were awarded the Pace CB Radio account and our first job was to make the brand stand out from the mass of CB radios that were flooding the market. Pace made very good radios but there wasn't anything remarkable that separated them from the competition. We would have to separate them somehow.

In working on the problem we decided that the best way to penetrate and separate would be with a humorous TV commercial. In our brainstorming sessions we came up with what we thought was a humorous— nay, silly—idea. What if an attractive waitress put out a call on her Pace CB and had a tremendous response? A really tremendous response.

The spot would start with a shot of the lovely "Lena, the Queen of Dan Ott's Diner" speaking on her Pace. The instant men heard her voice they would respond and begin racing to her—in cars, trucks, dune buggies, helicopters, on motorcycles, bicycles and any other vehicles we could think of. The client loved the storyboard we presented but then we faced a problem—we had to shoot it. It was an enormously complex—and expensive—shoot because in those pre-computer days we had to shoot all those real cars, dune buggies, helicopters, etc. on location.

Finding the diner where Lena made her call on her Pace CB

was the easy part. But rounding up all the vehicles the storyboard called for was another matter. And besides the vehicles, we needed a special-effects person to generate smoke from the tires as the vehicles peeled out to get to Lena as quickly as possible.

And finally, after much preparation, one morning we stood on a rural road north of Los Angeles with a director, camera crew and a small army of vehicles along with a two-seat helicopter. And so the shooting began. The task was to show the eye-popping (over)reaction of each driver upon hearing Lena's sexy voice and then their instant moving out. We kept the special effects man busy generating smoke for each peel-off.

As we came towards the end of the filming we faced a small problem—our special effects man was unhappy. Generating smoke wasn't really satisfying for him. What he really wanted to do was something special effects people are good at and apparently like to do—making an explosion. But as hard as we tried to satisfy him, we couldn't come up with a rational reason for having an explosion in the spot. So when we wrapped the shoot we all were very happy...except for our special effects expert who was visibly depressed.

When the commercial went on the air we found we had a hit on her hands. Everyone involved was happy—the client, the agency, the actors, the director.

The only one who wasn't happy was the special effects man. No explosion. No smile.

* * *

Facing tight deadlines, empty word processor screens, and conference rooms full of clients with "Show me, kid" written on their faces, being nervous was fairly common. But the word "scared" really fit only one incident that I can recall. And it was in a place I would normally love—in the cockpit of a jet.

As a private pilot, I loved any chance I got to fly on the job.

And this assignment was heavenly—my client, Western Airlines, had just added several new DC-10s to their fleet and we wanted to feature them in our commercials. It fell to me to fly aboard a jet that would film one of Western's DC-10s in flight. And so one day I found myself in a jet that was equipped to do in-flight filming. We were to rendezvous with the DC-10 at 10,000 feet over Palm Springs. The cameraman Bob and I sat before a 15-inch screen that showed what the camera was seeing, with him holding a button that started and stopped the filming.

I stared at the screen mesmerized as the DC-10 appeared in the distance. The captain of the DC-10 flew it as Bob directed and he started filming it at various angles and distances. After about ten minutes, he got the most dramatic shot of the day, a shot of the DC-10 so close that you could clearly see the pilot's mustache through his windscreen. I looked up from the camera screen and commented, "Your telephoto lens is terrific. The image is so crisp and clear. It's almost as if he's flying right next to us."

Bob responded, "That isn't a telephoto lens. And he is flying right next to us." And for the first time since the filming started I looked out the window. And I saw a sight that terrified me—the DC-10 was flying slightly below us so close that his left wing was flying under our plane. I had never been so close to another plane inflight in my life. My heart skipped several beats and it took me a minute or so to calm down.

I tried to cover up my terror but Bob saw through it and reassured me. I gradually calmed down and ended up loving that masterful flying.

When we landed, I thanked Bob for the adventure and the great air-to-air filming but parted with a friendly suggestion: get a telephoto lens.

* * *

Filming that DC-10 was a thrill. But what was even more thrilling was the time I piloted one.

I suppose I should clarify that somewhat. It was actually a DC-10 simulator sitting firmly on the ground inside the Western Airlines hangar at Los Angeles International Airport. I sat nervously in the pilot's left-hand seat looking over the complex instrument panel. Through the windscreen I saw the pilot's view of the world as the simulator placed me at 1,000 foot altitude approaching a simulated but very realistic runway.

I quickly found that flying a DC-10 was substantially different from flying a four-passenger Cessna 172. I flew the approach pattern with a lot of help from the instructor sitting in the right-hand seat. As my aircraft descended, my blood pressure ascended. I was doing it but not very well. We were never going to make it in one piece if I tried to complete the landing.

As we descended through 400 feet, my instructor gave up. With an emphatic "I've got it" he took over. I loved hearing the squeal of the simulated tires as they touched down on the simulated runway. As I mopped the non-simulated sweat from my brow, I had newfound respect for all the pilots who carry us safely through the sky. They make it look easy. But it isn't.

This practice didn't help me very much a few years later when I visited my son Gabe while he was attending the University of North Dakota studying to become an airline pilot. At one point he asked me if I would like to fly the simulator that they used in the pilot training course.

"I'd like it," I said confidently. After all I held my pilot's license and I had practiced on a Western Airlines simulator. What could go wrong?

I'll tell you what. As I was flying the approach to the simulator runway, the instrument panel started going berzerk and the view of the airport began bouncing around. We had hit some vicious turbulence. I couldn't control the plane and once again I heard my instructor in the right hand seat say, "I've got it."

He landed the plane safely and when I exited the simulator cockpit, I saw a strange sight—my son Gabe was standing there with an enormous grin splitting his face. In an instant I got it without him having to say a word. He had told the man controlling the simulation from a panel behind the cockpit to throw in some nasty turbulence for me. Nice.

I made Gabe pay for it. Or at least for our dinner that night.

* * *

There was nothing quite so heady to me in the world of advertising as when I stood on a set or location about to see my commercial idea come to life.

In contrast to the solo or duet performances that give birth to the commercial idea, actually shooting the spot is very much a group effort...a big group. There's the cast, the crew, agency people, clients. If there are children involved there are also social workers, teachers and nurses on hand. The problem is that a lot of those people want to see what's going on.

Today, that's easily solved. Most shoots are equipped with a system called video assist that sends the image both to the camera and to a video monitor. That way, everyone can see exactly what the cameraman is seeing. But in the days before video assist became available, the cameraman was the only one who saw the scene as it was being shot and so he had to be trusted implicitly. If he wasn't satisfied with the scene he had shot, he'd tell the director and they'd shoot it again.

When a scene is to be shot, the cameraman and director work together deciding on the angle, the framing of the scene, the kinds and timing of any camera moves, and all the other variables that contribute to the effectiveness of a shot. When the director is satisfied with the camera plan, they'll rehearse it until they're ready to shoot. At that point in the pre-video assist days, before the actual filming of a scene in a spot the director would invite someone, often the senior creative person on the set, to look through the viewfinder during a camera rehearsal to make sure the scene was satisfactory to him or her.

And so it happened that one day they were planning a shot that was extraordinarily complex. It started out with a tight close-up of an actor's face as he entered the room. The camera then was pulled back slowly so the view widened, the focus changing all the time to accommodate the other actor who entered the frame. Then the camera, which was on the end of a fifteen-foot metal crane and had started the scene at ground level, swung up fifteen feet into the air to capture the final seconds of the scene from a dramatic high angle.

It took five people to do the shot — the cameraman in a seat on the crane looking through the viewfinder to frame the shot, an assistant cameraman to maintain the constantly changing focus, another to control the zoom, a stagehand to pull the dolly back and another to raise the crane carrying the camera, cameraman and assistant to the heights. It was a half hour before the director felt confident enough to shoot the complex scene.

At that point, he invited me to "ride the shot"—take the cameraman's position and view a rehearsal of the scene to approve it before actually shooting it. To do that, I faced an arch nemesis of mine: the head on which the camera was mounted. It consisted of two wheels, one to pan the camera from side-to-side and another to point it up and down.

To me, controlling the camera with those damned wheels was like the good old pat-your-head-and-rub-your-tummy-then-switch trick. It had always been impossible for me to keep it straight—to pan right did I turn the front wheel clockwise or counterclockwise? Or was panning the other wheel? To tilt the camera down did I move that wheel toward me or away? And to do them both together at just the right time? Good luck, Cameraman Don.

When I sat in the cameraman's seat and looked through the

viewfinder, everything was set up for the opening tight close-up. I gripped the dreaded wheels as the director asked if I was ready. "Let's do it," I exclaimed with incredibly false bravado. Then the director announced, "This is a rehearsal folks....a-a-and Action!"

Everything started to happen at once...and much too quickly. The actor walked to the left, the frame widened, the focus changed, the other actor entered, the camera started flying upward. I spun my two wheels frantically trying to keep the scene framed.

Twelve seconds later I heard the blessed word "Cut!" and it was over. I knew that every one of the thirty pairs of eyes on the set was looking at me on the crane, now fifteen feet in the air. I was too embarrassed to take my eye away from the viewfinder. With my inept handling of those two control wheels, I had lost the action almost immediately and now, instead of the final wide shot looking down on two actors in a living room that I was supposed to be seeing, I had the camera pointing straight up at the ceiling of the studio. It was obvious to everyone in that big studio that I had really screwed up.

The director called up to me, his voice oozing with sarcasm. "The shot look okay, Don?"

"Looks great to me, Bill. Let's shoot it!"

My gang didn't let me forget it and that night I had to buy lots of drinks for my agency buddies, the cameraman and the director.

* * *

When I started in advertising in the early sixties, a big change was underway. Radio, once the mainstay of any advertising campaign, had already taken a back seat to television. But in ten years, another major innovation was going to shake up the world of advertising: the computer. And in some small way I may have helped that shakeup along...at least in Los Angeles.

"What the hell is a word processor?"

It was the very irritated voice of my boss, Jim Jordan, the Executive Creative Director of BBDO on the phone from New

York. I was the creative director of BBDO/West and had just asked him for $1,500 to buy a word processor for the typists in my creative department. The year was 1977 and the computer was virtually unknown let alone its offspring, word processors.

It had all started a few years earlier when my wife and I were visiting the home of a business associate and his wife. He showed me an interesting but puzzling piece of equipment. It was a metal box about as big as two shoeboxes and was connected to what looked like a small television screen along with a keyboard.

"It's called a computer," he explained. "Let me show you what it can do."

The screen was black and the letters on it were white. We played a very crude but fascinating game that had no graphics, just words displayed on the screen. Then he showed me a program he had written for the computer in a computer language called Basic. It was slow and clunky and I soon saw that the computer could do almost nothing. But for some reason I was mesmerized. After that evening, my wife and I visited these friends often, partially because of their hospitality, but mostly because of his computer.

The next Christmas my wife bought me the computer. The only difference between this one and my friend's was that mine was a do-it-yourself project. It came in thousands of pieces in a box and I had to build it from scratch. I had never so much as held a soldering iron but I fearlessly plugged mine in and slowly began to solder resistors (whatever they were) and transistors (whatever they were) and memory chips (whatever they were) to a motherboard (whatever that was) and after dozens of surprisingly enjoyable hours of soldering and construction, I plugged my grey box in and switched it on.

It worked. But the work it did was minimal. Today, even a modest computer will have a minimum of one million bytes of memory to work with. Mine had only four thousand bytes. But that was enough to keep me occupied for hours learning how to program in Basic. There was nothing productive about it, just a lot of mind-stretching fun learning a new language. It was something like doing crossword puzzles—at the end, you throw the puzzle you solved away. But it was a lot of fun getting there.

And little did I know what that grey box was going to do to my world of advertising.

* * *

My big eye-opening break in my new land of computerdom came when I visited another friend who had a similar computer. But he was doing more than solving simple puzzles or playing simple computer games. He was writing on his computer just as I had been writing my advertising on electric typewriters for years. But the difference was that when he made a mistake or wanted to change something, he just had to press some keys on the keyboard or use something called a mouse and the change was made.

As a writer, I was fascinated. I could make changes in something I wrote without all the cutting, pasting and brushing white goo on words and typing over them. It was called a word processor, my friend said. It was crude, a model T compared to today's word processors, but to me it was a miracle. I bought the word processing program for my computer and fell in love with it.

I discovered that not only was changing what I wrote easier but actually creating what I wrote seemed to come more easily. Because I knew that changing my work was so easy, I was less reluctant to put something down. Ideas appeared to flow better.

After using my word processor at home for several months, I asked the head secretary of my creative department to keep track of the kinds of typing they did for us. After two weeks, the statistics were stunning. Six out of every seven documents they typed were retyping previous documents. I worked the numbers in my head. How much time would our secretaries save if, instead of re-typing those six out of seven documents they used a word processor to just edit the original document on the keyboard? The time and labor savings would be enormous.

That was the genesis of that irritated "What the hell is a word processor?" response from my boss in New York when I asked for the money. I explained the word processor and told him about the results of my study and he reluctantly sprang for the money.

As crude as that early word processor was, it changed our world. It cut the workload and increased the productivity of everyone in the agency who had been chained to an electric typewriter for years. The change was dramatic. (And although we didn't know it at the time, the introduction of word processors was the foot-in-the-door for the even more revolutionary computers that were to follow.)

When I moved from BBDO/West to Foote Cone Belding, they were still in the world of electric typewriters. I spoke to the office head and convinced him to authorize the purchase of word processors for our creative department secretaries. When their word processors arrived, the two girls were obviously irritated by the prospect of having to learn how to use them. But I promised them it would make their lives easier.

Apparently it did. A week or so after the girls received their word processors and started using them, they walked into my office. And in their hands each of them held a rose for me.

It looked like the newfangled word processors I had gotten them were a hit after all.

∞ 12 ∞

ADVERTISING YOU'VE NEVER SEEN

If you've gotten this far, I'm sure you know that during my advertising career I've done work for numerous high-profile clients such as Xerox, AT&T, Jaguar, Bristol-Myers and ARCO. But some of the work I'm proudest of has been for smaller, less well-known companies. And rather than let that work go softly into the sunset without being seen I thought I'd showcase some of it as a finale to this book.

Is this a grand finale or a petite finale? You be the judge......

This client developed charitable foundations for wealthy people to help them save on taxes. At our agency, The Next Level, my partner Deborah Rodney and I faced a challenge: to create an ad that promoted those tax savings in a unique way. This brought a lot of smiles...and, more importantly, a lot of toll-free phone calls.

How do you convey the idea that your client is not just another typical investment banker? The cover of this brochure we created—all black and white except for the shoes—spoke volumes with almost no words. It contained a valuable element: the reader had to make the connection themselves between the word "different" and the work shoes. Once they did that and enjoyed their "Oh, I get it!" moment, we had won them.

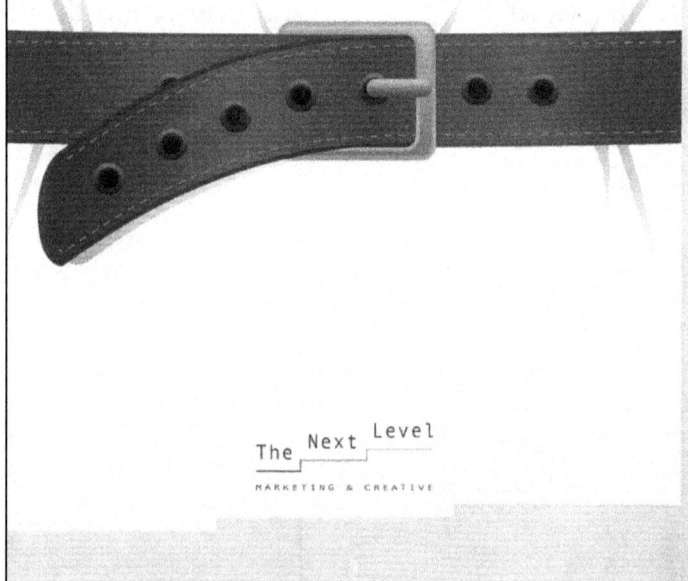

Deborah Rodney and I created this brochure to promote our agency, The Next Level, when the economy was suffering. Companies were cutting back on their marketing budgets and we believed that was the wrong way to go. We used this brochure to convince them…and to demonstrate how our creativity could cut through and get results. After all, they were reading this brochure weren't they?

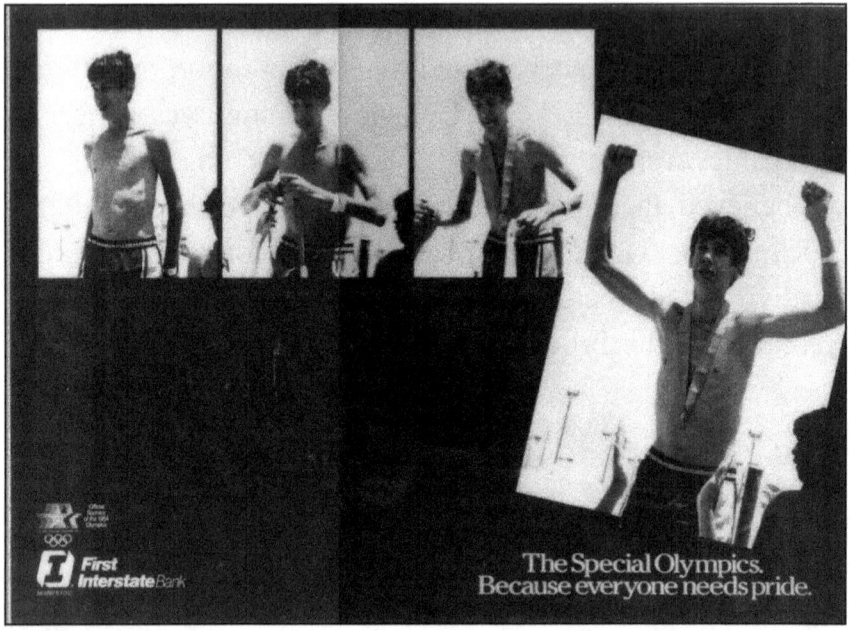

At Foote Cone Belding, we were charged with creating an ad for our client, First Interstate Bank, to be placed in the program of the 1983 Special Olympics. I remembered a series of pictures I had seen a few years earlier in the home of a client I was picking up for dinner. They were of her special-needs son who had competed in the Special Olympics and had won his race. I was very moved by the pictures and had never forgotten them. With this assignment I was thrilled to be able to use them.

The first thing our Master Blender ever smelled was whisky.

George Thompson

George Thompson's father was a workman in the storage sheds of the Johnnie Walker distillery in Kilmarnock, Scotland. His mother was a housemaid.

And since his mother's employers wouldn't permit her to bring little George with her to the manor house, at three months old he went to work with his father in a small wicker cradle.

For eight hours every day George breathed the clean, heather-soaked air that flowed through the sheds. And smelled the rich, crisp aroma of the whisky that sat mellowing in the barrels around him.

Years later, at just about the time the whisky that had surrounded George's cradle had matured enough to be bottled, George went to work for the distillery.

Today, George Thompson is the Master Blender at Johnnie Walker, responsible for ensuring that the famous light, smooth flavor of our whisky is constant from bottle to bottle, barrel to barrel, year to year.

Everyone marvels at how amazingly sensitive his nose is, especially when it comes to judging whisky. But George doesn't think his sense of smell is anything special. It's just that he started using it a bit earlier than most people.

The Scotch that made Scotch.

Johnnie Walker was the second Scotch whisky account I worked on...and the second one that I didn't get to go to Scotland to do research on. But the research I did do via books and interviews was interesting and turned up some very fascinating facts. One of them was that their Master Blender at the time was actually born in a distillery. This ad was the result.

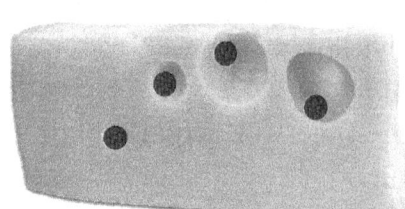

Generation IX, an internet security firm, had an excellent record of protecting their clients from bad guys who wanted to violate their network, stealing data or doing damage in other potentially costly ways. We believed that the best way to gain the interest of prospects would be to scare them by pointing out the dangers their network faced. This postcard we created had a simple but unique feature --- we punched holes in the cheese. They made all the difference. In follow-up phone calls, every single prospect remembered the postcard with the holes.

It was big news in 1963 when the U.S. and Russia installed the Hot Line—a direct connection between The White House and Moscow. With this in place, it was believed that the chance of an event being misinterpreted as hostile could be defused immediately. Our client, ITT, had installed and maintained the line. When a carrier launch during the Arab-Israel war appeared threatening to Russia, the Hot Line was used to assure Premier Kosygin that the event was innocent. This ad made that story public for the first time.

Whoever said conventions are fun never had to plan one.

A great convention: the meetings are enlightening, the dinners fattening, and the parties embarrassing.

But who puts it all together — the hotel reservations, airline tickets, hall rental, catering…? If you're the one who does it, you're probably doing it wrong. Because you could have Western Airlines Convention Coddlers doing it all for you…at no extra charge.

Call Western to help with your next meeting or convention and we'll do a lot more than just sell you tickets on Western. We'll arrange for rooms, ground transportation, banquets, audio-visual aids, sightseeing…anything and everything to make your convention very unconventional.

Let Western arrange your next convention and someone will enjoy it who you never thought would: you.

Western Airlines
The Convention Coddlers

I've laughed at and loved Laurel and Hardy ever since I was a toddler. In the '60's, at the suggestion of a fellow copywriter in New York, I wrote to Stan in California and got a warm, friendly letter in reply from him which I still treasure. Several years later, when I got an assignment to advertise a special convention-planning service of our client, I remembered a movie the boys had done and was delighted to be able to use this still from it.

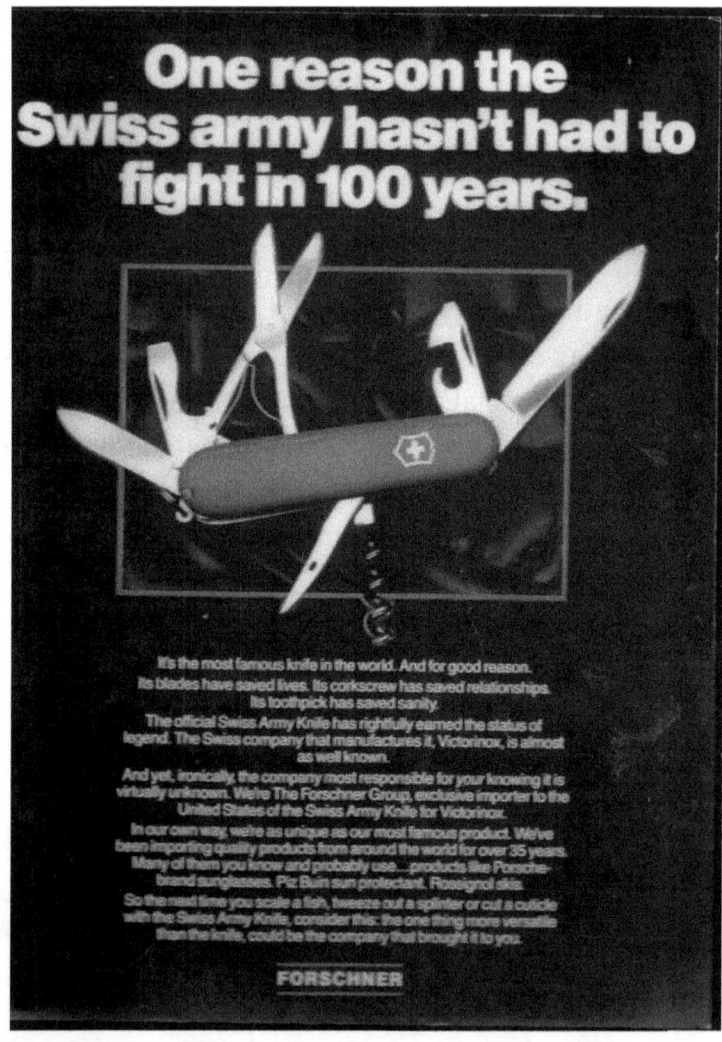

When we got their account, our client's product was very famous but the company itself was virtually unknown. Forschner was the exclusive importer of the Swiss Army Knife. Our job was to raise awareness of the company. This ad capitalized on their famous knife so that some of that fame would rub off on them.

Las Vegas 33% off: no shit.

—— Starting June 1, ——

And finally—this ad I did for Western Airlines promoting a special fare to Las Vegas never made it to print…but I sure wish it had.

You can't win 'em all.

About the author

With an advertising career that actually started on Madison Avenue, Don Spector qualifies as a genuine Mad Man.

His advertising debut was anything but spectacular. Armed with a bachelor's degree in psychology and a master's in finance, he started in a $50-a-week mailroom job in a Madison Avenue ad agency. While delivering mail to the agency creative director one day, he slipped in some homework he had done for a copywriting course he had taken. A few days later he sat proudly at a desk with a new title: junior copywriter.

Fortunately for him, the agency had a number of high-profile accounts like Tareyton cigarettes and Smirnoff Vodka. It was a good opportunity to create ads and commercials for products that were highly visible and his rise in advertising's creative world began.

Over the next decades he worked in several agencies creating advertising for accounts like AT&T's Yellow Pages, Bristol-Myers and Jaguar. His portfolio of work was noted and he received an offer to move to Los Angeles to BBDO/West where he ultimately became creative director.

From there, he moved to Foote Cone Belding L.A, But the entrepreneurial bug soon bit him and he ultimately left the major agency world to become a principal in his own agency.

Millions have seen his TV commercials and print advertising for clients like Xerox, ARCO, Absolut Vodka and dozens more.

A Final Word from the Author

I hope you've enjoyed my *"Memories."* As you've read, my adventures in the world of advertising were at various times fascinating, funny, satisfying, infuriating…(add any adjectives you like. They all fit.)

I've told many of these stories over the years but had no idea that people were interested in advertising until the show *"Mad Men."* The overwhelming success of the series made me realize that I wasn't just an ad guy…starting on Madison Avenue at the same time the show's story began, I was a real Mad Man so people might like to read my stories. And this book was born.

I invite you to review the book on the platform you purchased it. And I'd enjoy hearing from you. I promise to respond.

Email: dspector250@gmail.com
Facebook: www.facebook.com/don.spector

Best wishes,

Don

Don Spector

www.ingramcontent.com/pod-product-compliance
Lightning Source LLC
Chambersburg PA
CBHW051905170526
45168CB00001B/245